W0246481

UNDERCOVER
KINDNESS

UNDERCOVER KINDNESS

Saying Yes to Love,
No to Fear,
and Embracing the
Life-Changing Power of
Ordinary Generosity

Jimmy Darts
with Jamie Blaine

CONVERGENT BOOKS
NEW YORK, NY

Convergent
An imprint of Random House
A division of Penguin Random House LLC
1745 Broadway, New York, NY 10019
convergentbooks.com
penguinrandomhouse.com

Unless otherwise indicated, Scripture quotations are taken from the New King James Version®. Copyright © 1982 by Thomas Nelson. Used by permission. All rights reserved.

Scripture quotations marked (AMP) are taken from the Amplified® Bible, copyright © 2015 by The Lockman Foundation. Used by permission. (www.lockman.org).

Scripture quotations marked (KJ21) are taken from the 21st Century King James Version®, copyright © 1994 by Deuel Enterprises, Inc., Gary, South Dakota 57237. All rights reserved.

Scripture quotations marked (NIV) are taken from the Holy Bible, New International Version®, NIV®. Copyright © 1973, 1978, 1984, 2011 by Biblica Inc.™ Used by permission of Zondervan. All rights reserved worldwide. (www.zondervan.com). The "NIV" and "New International Version" are trademarks registered in the United States Patent and Trademark Office by Biblica Inc.®

Scripture quotations marked (NLT) are taken from the Holy Bible, New Living Translation, copyright © 1996, 2004, 2015 by Tyndale House Foundation. Used by permission of Tyndale House Publishers, Carol Stream, Illinois 60188. All rights reserved.

Scripture quotations marked (TPT) are taken from The Passion Translation®. Copyright © 2017, 2018, 2020 by Passion & Fire Ministries Inc. Used by permission. All rights reserved. (ThePassionTranslation.com).

Copyright © 2025 by Jimmy Darts, LLC

All photos courtesy of the author.

Penguin Random House values and supports copyright. Copyright fuels creativity, encourages diverse voices, promotes free speech, and creates a vibrant culture. Thank you for buying an authorized edition of this book and for complying with copyright laws by not reproducing, scanning, or distributing any part of it in any form without permission. You are supporting writers and allowing Penguin Random House to continue to publish books for every reader. Please note that no part of this book may be used or reproduced in any manner for the purpose of training artificial intelligence technologies or systems.

CONVERGENT with colophon is a registered trademark of Penguin Random House LLC.

Hardcover ISBN 978-0593-73595-4
Ebook ISBN 978-0593-73596-1

Printed in the United States of America on acid-free paper

2 4 6 8 9 7 5 3 1

1st Printing

First Edition

BOOK TEAM: Production editor: Cassie Gitkin • Managing editor: Allison Fox
Production manager: Kevin Garcia • Copy editor: Sheryl Rapée-Adams
Proofreaders: Rachael Clements, Marissa Earl, Andrea Gordon, Emily Zebrowski

Book design by Jo Anne Metsch

The authorized representative in the EU for product safety and compliance is Penguin Random House Ireland, Morrison Chambers, 32 Nassau Street, Dublin D02 YH68, Ireland.
https://eu-contact.penguin.ie

I dedicate this book to all the undercover heroes heaven won't stop talking about—the ones sowing seeds of His love in grocery aisles, parking lots, and gas stations. You may not have a stage, but angels are on the edge of their seats, watching you and cheering you on.

You're walking sermons in sneakers. Never water down the gospel. Don't believe the lie that you were meant to just get by—always struggling with sin or barely scraping by financially. No, you were made to soar. To thrive. To carry the joy and freedom Jesus paid for. To light up dark places with grace, leaving trails of hope like confetti.

And remember: God multiplies what you steward. If you desire to carry more for Him, take care of what's already in your hands. Stewardship unlocks greater assignments.

Contents

Prologue 3

I: HEARTS 5

The First Blind Car Salesman in the State
    of Arizona 7

Down at the Fresh Start Laundromat 15

I've Been Used to Pain 19

II: DARTS 25

Flip Cams, Family Restaurants, and Praying
    for the Stranger at Table Five 27

Please, Jesus, Give Me a Crazy Life 34

God Healed My Socks 43

Are You Sure? 46

The Life-Changing Power of Fun 54

Town Fool 62

Life to the Fullest 69

III: WHAT'S COOKIN' 77

Undeniable Touch 79

Miracles Beneath the Mount Everest
    of Trash 84

Flushing Hell 93

Keep Austin Weird 100

That One Moment When I Knew What I
    Was Called to Do 108

Your Idol Is Finally Dead 111

IV: LIL' BIT OF KINDNESS 119

This Is How You Start 121

No Security 131

Best Friends for the Day 140

V: OHH, BABY 147

The Kindness Challenge 149

Purity, Not Perfection 154

Give Steve a Chance 158

The Lights Are Green 165

Hell's Scared 170

Lil' Bit of Heaven Broke Loose 176

VI: WHAT THE HECK 185

See Everything Happy 187

A Donkey, a Burning Bush, or Even Me? 196

Yes Is Yes Forever 204

VII: THAT'S CANDY 207

Help You More Than It Hurts Me 209

Joy Is So Contagious 215

Peaceful and Wild 219

Just Help One 223

See What He Will Do 229

Thank You, Everybody! 233

UNDERCOVER
KINDNESS

Prologue

Write the vision and make it plain . . .
that he may run who reads it.

—HABAKKUK 2:2

SUMMER 2020

"Jimmy, what do you want to *do* with your life?"

My dad was sitting on our back deck looking out over the rippling waters of Leech Lake, and by the tone of his voice, I could tell he meant business. I was twenty-three years old, back waiting tables at his restaurant in small-town Minnesota, feeling like Moses in the desert, still wandering in circles when I was way beyond ready to arrive.

I'd been a dog walker, mousetrap entrepreneur, and failed YouTuber. I'd gone through missionary training, supernatural ministry school, a nine-month super-intensive Bible study, planting churches in Texas, mission trips around the world . . . and here I was, back serving chicken-fried steak and taco salads again, feeling no closer to my purpose and calling than I did before. It was time for a change.

"You mean if I could do anything?" I asked.

My dad nodded. I leaned closer and asked again.

"*Anything?*"

I

Hearts

The First Blind Car Salesman in the State of Arizona

Joy is a net of love by which you can catch souls.

—MOTHER TERESA

WINTER 2023

I was scrolling through TikTok one night when a video caught my eye. A news reporter in Mesa, Arizona, told a story about Sebastian, a blind and partially deaf man who'd been selling brooms, mops, and other items by the side of the road since 2015. Sebastian had many obstacles to overcome. He'd been cheated and given counterfeit bills by would-be customers. Some even stole his brooms.

When cancer attacked his wife, Sebastian started working twice as hard to support his family. Then he lost his van in an accident. (Don't worry, Sebastian wasn't driving.) It became a struggle to transport his supply. Sales fell off and his family was evicted from their home.

Still, Sebastian pressed on, depending on the kindness of strangers and friends to help get his merchandise around. "In hot weather, I sell popsicles, and when it's cold, I sell blankets," he told the reporter. "Giving up is not in my vocabulary. If God needs me to be a blind guy with a great attitude, that's what I'll be."

I threw some clothes in a bag and headed off to Arizona to buy a broom. Sebastian was at his post on the corner of McKellips and Mesa Drive. "Hello, sir," I said. "How much for the brooms?"

"I got one for six or two for ten bucks," he replied. "It's my Black Friday deal."

"Wasn't Black Friday like, three months ago?"

"Yeah, but every day is black to me." He pretended to look around, selling a joke I'm sure he'd told a thousand times before. It was still funny. You couldn't help but love this guy.

I made my pitch. "Is there any way you could do one broom for five?"

"Five dollars?" he asked, looking hurt.

"Sorry," I said. "That's all I got on me."

Another sad pause. I was asking to see if Sebastian would give me a deal, knowing that if the internet saw this man, despite all his circumstances, helping me, it could inspire them to rally behind him in unimaginable ways and ultimately change his life. His responses were breaking my heart though, and I nearly blew it and gave in. But he let me off the hook, lighting up the street with his smile. "Okay, man!" he said. "Let's do it."

Wow. Good salesman. We exchanged my five-dollar bill for his broom. I ran my fingers over the bright purple bristles. As brooms go, it was a nice one. "How'd you get in the broom business?" I asked.

"No one would hire me because I was blind," he replied. "So, I created my own job."

Sebastian told me about his family: two young children and a wife battling to get well again so she could help out. The Bible says a prayer offered in faith heals the sick and lifts the brokenhearted. I want to give and help and listen, but I always ask if it's okay to pray.

"Of course," Sebastian said as I took his hand. "Prayer is more important than money any day."

"Well, guess what?" I said after we prayed. "Because you helped me today, I got a thousand dollars for you right here."

I pulled the bills from my pocket. Ten hundred-dollar bills fluttering in the desert wind. He probably thought I was joking. I handed them over and waited until he'd closed his fist tight to let go.

He ran his fingers through the stack. "Oh. Ohhh . . ." Sebastian said, slowly realizing it wasn't a setup. "Oh! Can I have a hug?"

I threw my arms around him and we clapped each other on the back.

"So, you're selling brooms because you couldn't get a job," I said. "What's your dream job?"

He smiled again, this time with a hint of mischief. "I want to be the first blind car salesman in the state of Arizona."

.   .   .

There are all kinds of people in the world, dreaming all kinds of dreams. I once had a dream, too, and I believe firmly that when your dreams start to come true, it's your turn to help somebody else reach theirs. I had to wonder though, *A blind car salesman? How's that gonna work? What car lot is going to take a chance on someone who can't drive or see the inventory?*

I posted a video showcasing Sebastian's kindness, which racked up millions of views. The GoFundMe I created brought in over one hundred thousand dollars overnight. The next afternoon, I planned to go back to Sebastian's corner to do a follow-up video telling him about the money people had given after watching his story.

An idea struck. Sebastian had been selling brooms in Mesa for nearly eight years. He was well known in the community, beloved for his humor and positive attitude.

I sent out a quick post saying that I'd be surprising Sebastian in a couple of hours, asking locals to come out and join in the surprise. I didn't know if anyone would show up on such short notice.

When I walked up to that corner, I couldn't even see Sebastian or his brooms because so many people were gathered around him, a whole flash mob of compassion holding up elaborate handmade signs with messages of love and support. One woman even made shirts. Mesa's news crew was there to make sure plenty of others also heard his story.

I weaved through the people to him. "Whoa, Sebastian!" Another big hug. "Look at *this*!"

The crowd spontaneously lined up to buy brooms. Everybody. Even little kids queued up clutching ten-dollar bills to put in Sebastian's hand.

"There's a line?" he said. "I've never had a line."

When things settled down, I gave him the news. "People all over the world saw your story and they want to help you out! You now have over a hundred thousand dollars and it's all for you and your family."

"WE LOVE YOU, SEBASTIAN!" the crowd cheered.

The street corner comic who was never at a loss for words had none at that moment. All he could do was stand there, trying to take it all in.

"A hundred thousand . . . dollars?" he finally said, a huge smile taking over his face. "Thank you, thank you, thank you . . ."

But the surprises weren't done. After one man bought a mop, he caught the salesman's sleeve. "Sebastian, I want to offer you a job selling cars."

We were all speechless. I had no clue that was going to happen! Sebastian threw his arms in the air and everyone started whooping and hollering. Right there on a street corner in downtown Mesa, Arizona, we all began to dance.

·　　·　　·

Heyyy, reader, what's cookin'? I'm Jimmy Darts.

Maybe you've seen me doing kindness challenges on social media. I travel to thrift shops, laundromats, street corners, and grocery stores across the country trying to find one Good Samaritan who's willing to help a stranger. I'll ask for fifty cents to buy a Mother's Day card or if I can practice my face painting on them for my upcoming booth at the county fair. I'll see if someone—anyone— will help push my beat-up Honda to the corner gas station. I get a lot of confused looks and noes . . . but it's all worth it when that one person steps up and gives, often when they don't even have enough for themselves.

My work has taken me all over this country, and I've

learned that there are a lot of awesome, generous, nice, cool, kindhearted people out there. In blue states and red, rich and poor, north and south—everywhere—there are people like Sebastian, making kindness a habit and showing that there's a goodness in us that's bigger than all the crazy stuff that tears us apart. Most of these people have been paying it forward their whole lives, but no one's noticed. This is their moment. I believe God notices, and I want the world to know.

In the upcoming pages, I'll tell stories of some of the amazing people I've met along the way and the unbelievable experiences that convinced me that this world and people in general aren't as harsh as we are led to believe. It turns out, mean people often need the biggest hugs. The people you hate or dislike out there—well, guess what? God made them too. There's gold inside of them. It might just be buried under the weight of life's circumstances or how they were raised. But if you can love them enough to love the hell out of them, you might see their life transform in ways you never imagined. And you'll be amazed at the unexpected friendships you'll make along the way.

What God has done in someone else's life, He can do in yours. That doesn't mean we're all going to have the same haircut, the same job, or the same stories to write about. But it does mean that if we yield to Him, have enough faith, live with joy, embrace fun, and keep our hearts available, God can take each of us on our own unique path. He'll fulfill the destiny He's created us for in ways we can't even imagine.

I'll also be sharing more about faith than I do in my videos. There's a reason for that—well, you'll see later in the book . . . but basically, that's my "anything," the answer to my dad's question all those years ago. My life, so far, has been a journey in believing that God is good, never taking no for an answer, and refusing to live a small, boring life.

You may not be the kind of person who's comfortable asking strangers for food, and you might not have an extra hundred dollars to give to the first person who says yes. No kind act is unimportant. You can start the same way I did: right where you are with what you have to give.

So, let's go!

Down at the Fresh Start Laundromat

Whatever a man sows, that he will also reap.

—APOSTLE PAUL

"Hey, you should make a video here in Riverside," my best friend Ray said.

We were passing through and the truth is, I didn't want to make another video. The pressure to constantly create and share on social media can fry your brain and there are times when I just don't have the energy or inspiration for it.

Then again, every time we make one, it changes someone's life. Not just the person in the video. It changes the people who watch it too.

If you pray to make a difference and help people, you should know that there will be times when you won't feel inspired or enthusiastic. But if you say that prayer in good faith, it means you do it anyway, even when you don't feel like it.

"All right," I told Ray. "Let's find a laundromat and ask somebody for help."

Who doesn't love watching clothes spin in a circle? So, I figured we'd go to a laundromat and see if we could find someone there who needed help.

Ray and I drove all around Riverside, trying to find one that felt right. Too busy. Empty. Too loud. We must have hit about thirteen laundromats, praying and looking around.

"Okay, let's try one more," I told him. I was ready to go home.

We pulled up to a strip mall laundromat. A lady was sorting through her clothes while dressed in a gray hoodie and pink sweatpants, her hair in long, tight braids. She looked exhausted but kind.

I walked up to her with an armload of wadded-up clothes I'd fished from my back seat. "Excuse me, ma'am?" I said. "Do you have a couple extra quarters at all? For some soap?"

"I don't, I just spent my last," she said. "But I can give you some soap."

When she smiled and handed me a Tide Pod, my attitude did a 180. "You can have this for helping me," I said, handing her a piece of my laundry.

"It's your shirt?" she asked cautiously, probably thinking it was a prank. Carefully unfolding it, she found five hundred dollars in twenty-dollar bills. Her face changed from suspicious to confused. "What?" she said. One big tear spilled down her cheek. "Are you kidding?"

"What's your name?" I asked.

"Shelly."

"You're amazing, Shelly," I said. "Thank you for helping me today."

Shelly did not want to take the money. "No, please, give this to someone else. There are people who need this more than me."

Turns out Shelly had slept the last few nights in her car. After a job fell through, she'd been couch surfing, trying to figure out a plan. "I haven't been in a good place," she confessed. "Not at all."

I told Shelly that if she was the kind of person who'd give a stranger some soap to wash their clothes, even when she was struggling, God would be faithful to help her too. I promised that I would be praying.

We hugged by the tumbling clothes dryers and then Ray and I got back in the car. "When you're behind, it's hard to catch up," I told him as we drove away. "To get an apartment, you need a down payment. To get a job, you gotta get the right clothes. Five hundred dollars isn't enough. She's gonna need more."

We raised twenty-three thousand dollars for Shelly. Millions of people saw the same thing in her that God showed me. They got to partner in the work, in the blessing. They got to help Shelly make a new start.

A few weeks later, she reached out. "I got a job!"

I pulled up to the apartment complex where Shelly said she'd meet me. I walked in through the foyer and looked around. A beautiful, well-dressed woman sat at the welcome desk. "Jimmy!" she said, jumping up to meet me at the door.

"Shelly?"

Holy buckets! I've seen a few transformations, but this was incredible. Shelly had gotten an apartment, a job as a leasing agent, and even a new cat to keep her company.

"I don't know how you found me that day," she said. "But I am so thankful."

"Aw, me too," I told her with a shrug.

I've Been Used to Pain

The LORD is near to those who have a broken heart.

—PSALM 34:18

I was passing through Minneapolis when I saw this guy shooting baskets by himself in a church parking lot. I kept driving, but something pulled me back, like a spotlight was shining on him from above.

I turned the car around and wheeled into the next lot over. He was a tall, lanky fellow wearing a black hoodie tucked into too-short pajama pants with a pair of . . . gray Crocs? Hooping in Crocs? My kinda guy.

As I was walking up, his basketball rebounded off the rim and bounced my way. I scooped it up and tossed it back to him. "Hey, man," I said, "I was gonna come hoop here too, but someone stole my ball."

"Oh, for real?" he replied.

"Yeah, yeah," I said. "You mind if I shoot with you for a little bit?"

"I got no problem with that." He held out his fist for a bump. "Reggie."

"Jimmy," I said, bumping fists. "Good to meet you, man."

We sank a few. Bank shots, baseline floaters, fade-aways, and corner threes. He was good, nailing way more shots than me. "You play anywhere?" I asked.

"Right now, I'm training for G League." G League is the NBA's development league program. It's where many pro players get their start.

Shoot. Swish. He continued. "I went to college for a year, but I had some family stuff going on . . ."

On the front of Reggie's hoodie, there was a picture of a person about his age with ALWAYS LOVING written in tribute above and below. "Aw, man, I just noticed your shirt. Someone passed away?"

He lowered the basketball, head down. "Yeah," he said. "My homie died a couple of months back."

"Sorry to hear that."

Reggie nodded and passed me the ball. We kept shooting back and forth. "I just feel like the sun's gonna come out through those clouds," I told him. "You know?"

"It definitely is," he agreed. "I'm waiting for it."

I handed the ball back to him. "Here, hold this for a second?"

I pulled out my wallet. "Hey, bro, because you were

so kind to let me shoot with you, I got five hundred dollars for you," I said, fanning out the bills.

Reggie stared at the money, shaking his head like maybe it was some kind of trick.

"Appreciate you," I said, handing him the cash. "Just rewarding kindness."

Reggie looked off into the clouds, still shaking his head. "That's heaven-sent," he said softly. "Like, crazy. It's the wildest timing. I'm still trying to comprehend."

Reggie told me he had been bouncing around, in and out of shelters, staying at different people's houses since he was thirteen. "It ain't nothing new to me," he said. "I've been used to pain. Sadness makes me happy. Happiness makes me happier."

Reggie was a good guy with a lot of life and light in his eyes, even though he'd been through some tough times. "Your past isn't your future," I told him. "God's gonna use you to change young men's lives. You're not going to live on the street—you're going to get people off the street. I believe in you, brother. And God does too."

We exchanged numbers. Since Reggie was from Minneapolis and we were about the same age, I asked if he remembered a giant event for teens called WE Day at the Xcel Energy Center. "When I was a senior in high school, I stormed the stage unannounced and gave a speech."

"No way, that was *you*?" he asked. "I was there! You were that dude who said you wanted to change this country for the better."

"Yep," I replied. "And then security caught me and made me call my principal. They kicked me out of school."

We laughed and then I said, "Hey, before I go, what's your dream shoe?"

When I got back to the car, I whipped out my phone and started calling local shoe stores. "Do you have any Kyries in a size thirteen?"

Call after call. *Nope.* Kyrie Irving Nikes were an insanely popular shoe. Finally, a salesclerk said, "I got one pair left, but you better hurry 'cause we close in twenty minutes."

Reggie's video caught fire and his GoFundMe brought in twenty thousand dollars overnight. I messaged him to meet the next day and walked up with the Nike box in my hand. "Here you go, bro," I said.

Reggie opened the box, pulled one sneaker out of the paper, and looked it over like it was the keys to a solid gold Ferrari. "You got my dream shoes?" he asked. "For real?"

"Yeah, but that's not all," I told him. "Last night, people from around the world saw your story and contributed. We want to help you out with twenty thousand dollars to chase your dreams."

"Huh?"

Reggie stood there with a confused look on his face. I guess it was a lot to take in. There was still one more surprise. "One of the viewers hit me up with a G League contact. They want to help you get a tryout."

Reggie just walked away. I don't know if he was in tears, shock, or both. It's that feeling when it's been dark for a long time and you finally see the sun. You hope and pray for things to change, but a part of you is sure they never will. And then one day . . .

Over the next few days, the money kept coming in. NBA players messaged Reggie, offering encouragement. ESPN called, asking if Reggie and I would be on the closing segment of *NBA Today*.

They replayed the original video and follow-up clip, asking for our thoughts.

"If you have a dream, keep it going," I told the viewers. "Everyone has gold inside. Sometimes that gold can be covered up by the hard things in life. Deep down, you just need someone to believe in you. Even if you can't find someone to believe in you, God does, and that's all you need. So, don't give up."

Reggie told ESPN that he was getting ready for a

tryout, but in the meantime had started college and was studying hard to get his degree in business administration.

NBA Today let Reggie have the last word. "I hope people see that it's real. Keep grinding, keep trying, keep fighting. Someone in this world is going to see you. Everything can change in a day."

.   .   .

ESPN wasn't the only outlet wanting to talk. As my content gathered major worldwide traffic, podcasts and YouTubers reached out, curious about who I was and how it all began.

"So, how'd you get into creating videos and doing the undercover kindness thing?" one interviewer asked. "What's the story behind that?"

"Well, yeah, you see," I began, sorting it out in my head. "Truth is, it all started when I was ten . . ."

II

Darts

Flip Cams, Family Restaurants, and Praying for the Stranger at Table Five

If you're too big to serve, you're too small to lead.

—RICH WILKERSON JR.

I grew up in Walker, Minnesota, a town of a thousand people two hours south of the Canadian border. We didn't have a McDonald's, a movie theater, or even a Walmart. The only thing to do in Walker was hang out at the lake in the summer. (And for fun during winter, we'd hang out by the frozen lake and try not to die of hypothermia because the temperature was twenty below.)

I went to a small Lutheran school and my family belonged to a little nondenominational church called Living Water. Pastor Rick was our next-door neighbor. It was a good, all-American kind of life. But even as a kid, I was always looking for something bigger.

Christmas 2005, I found it. Or at least a place to start.

I was ten that year, and on Christmas morning, my mom, dad, and two older sisters, Brooke and Chelsie, were gathered around the tree. My parents gave me two hundred dollars with the condition that I could keep one hundred but had to give the other away. There was also a small box with my name on it.

I ripped off the wrapping paper to find the latest in technology: the Flip Video Camera, a pocket-size device that, according to the package, made videos "simple to shoot, simple to share." This was before cellphone cameras, but after those bulky units my dad's generation used to lug around on their shoulders to make a video.

The Flip cam was the OG YouTuber camera, featuring a big lens on the front and a tiny screen on the back side with a few simple buttons around it. The video quality was something like 420 pixels, so muddy and pixelated that if the action was intense, it looked like you were filming Lego people through a screen door. To share the videos, you had to flip out the USB arm, hook the Flip cam to your computer, and wait about seventeen hours while it transferred a forty-second clip. (It didn't really take that long, but it sure felt that way when I was ten.)

I must have made fifty videos that Christmas. I ran around our house filming everything, messing with my sisters, playing pranks on my mom, and scaring my cousin while he was asleep.

My mom had a manger scene set up for the holidays. I stole Baby Jesus, carried Him up to my room, and shot a video with my other toys. Our little Lord Jesus was no longer asleep in the hay. And He could talk! In a funny voice!

Baby Jesus foiled Captain Hook's scheme to rob the First Bank of Walker. Hook returned in the next episode with a rotten plan to pawn off crocodiles in vengeance for his missing hand. However, the wicked captain was no match for Baby Jesus as He overcame evil with the forces of good once again.

.   .   .

Remember that two hundred dollars I got for Christmas? My brain started spinning big toy dreams: Game Boy Color, Razor Kick, Hot Wheels 4-Loop track that climbed the wall . . .

"Remember, one hundred is for you to spend on whatever you want," my mom said. "The other is for you to give away to help someone."

Oh, dang. Okay.

After the holidays, my mom would drive me and my sisters to the Mall of America, in Minneapolis, to shop for school clothes. It was the largest mall in the country, with a Camp Snoopy amusement park inside.

Mall of America sits just south of Minneapolis. As we made our way through town, I noticed a man was hunched against the guardrail, trying to hide from the cruel Minnesota wind.

"Hey, Mom, stop," I said, pointing out the window. "I wanna give my hundred dollars to him."

Our car was headed for the on-ramp to the freeway and there was no place to pull over or park. My mom ran two tires up on the median and I rolled the window down. As the man walked over, cars started piling up behind us, everybody honking.

"Here you go, sir," I said, pulling the money from my sweatpants pocket and holding it out. "This is for you."

He looked up at me. His face was weathered and raw from the wind, hair straggly and gray. I'd never seen a homeless person up close before. For a split second, he just stared at me. I imagine he was used to getting loose change and dirty looks and here was some little suburban kid holding out a crisp one-hundred-dollar bill. At first, he looked shook. Then he lit up with a smile.

"God bless," he said, reaching to take the money. "Thank you so much."

"God bless you too," I told him. "Jesus loves you."

I rolled my window up, stoked, feeling like I could fly. Helping that man was more of a thrill than any mall roller coaster could offer. Better than any Hot Wheels track or video game. I don't even remember what I bought with my leftover hundred that year, but I'll never forget that moment.

Growing up in church and Christian school, I was taught the importance of giving and serving others. But there's a part of it you'll never understand until you see the look in someone's eyes when you change their life, even if that change is just for one day or one hour. With the money I gave that homeless man, he could buy a warm jacket and some food. Maybe he could even find a place to sleep inside.

I thought about my homeless friend a lot after that. When I lay in my warm bed at night, I wondered where he was sleeping. When my belly was full after dinner, I wondered what he had eaten that day. I wished I had given him my other hundred dollars too.

I started to notice people all the time, on street corners and park benches, pushing shopping carts filled with everything they owned, women wrapped in newspapers and dirty tarps, hiding from the cold, hiding from those who might judge them. How would you feel if you were judged at your lowest point?

"Whatever you do for the least of My brothers and sisters, you do for Me," Jesus said.

I wanted to do more for others and God. A lot more. But how?

.   •   •

Saturday morning at my house. I'm eating Froot Loops and watching cartoons with my feet kicked up on the footstool when the phone rings. I freeze with my spoon in mid-bite, dribbling milk, waiting for the bad news from Jimmy's Family Restaurant to hit.

"James!" My mom calls from the kitchen. "Go get in the car. They need another roller."

When your family owns a restaurant, there are no child labor laws. Washing dishes, wiping off tables, cutting the grass out back. I rolled a ton of silverware.

Eventually, I moved up to seating guests and handing out menus until my dad put me on the fryers because nothing could go wrong. You literally just pull french fries in and out of a greasy basket. Until I found out I was on soup duty too. I'm left-handed and would spill soup everywhere.

"Out of the kitchen!" my dad yelled. "Go do a lot check!" That meant I had to walk up and down the parking lot picking up any cigarette butts or trash on the ground. If I left even one out there, he'd know because our parking lot was so spotless. (By the way, the "Jimmy" in Jimmy's Restaurant isn't me. My grandpa is Jim Kellogg Sr. I'm Jimmy number two.)

One day my dad handed me an apron. "Congratulations, James," he said, slapping me on the back. "You're a busboy now."

When I got older, I moved to other areas of the restaurant. Waiting tables was a lot harder, but it was more money too. I had to learn to be fast and friendly while taking down complex orders, like the mom in section two wants a taco salad with extra cheese, her son is allergic to peanuts, and the lady at the counter would like a Diet Pepsi with no ice.

The problem was, I couldn't even read my own handwriting—let alone the cooks' in the kitchen. Because I was left-handed, my hand would drag ink across the sheet as I wrote and it looked like chicken scratch.

Please, Jesus, Give Me a Crazy Life

Indecision, in itself, is a choice. It's either the world and its
pleasures and its gods or it's Christ. Which is it for you?

—BILLY GRAHAM

Once I hit seventh grade, I had to transfer to Walker
High. I had been the loud, funny, crazy, outgoing kid in
my small Lutheran school where I only had four other
classmates, but once I showed up to a class where there
were a hundred kids in the grade, I was a lot shyer and felt
like hiding under a bush. Also, I had scoliosis and walked
pigeon-toed because my left leg was shorter than my
right one.

"Hey, Crooked-Foot!" one Walker High bully yelled.
I turned to look, and he was exaggerating the way I
walked. The other kids all laughed. I felt horrible, but
then I realized that when a bully says something, it's often
because they're getting bullied at home. So, I learned not
to take it to heart too much. And long story short, several

years after I graduated, I ran into the kid and we were able to shake it off and become buds. Everything worked out, but before then, I still tried my best to walk as straight as I could with my foot.

My mom took me to multiple doctors and chiropractors, trying to find someone to help me walk better and not hurt so much. Eventually we found a doctor who told us there was an option, one small glimmer of hope. Orthopedic surgeons could perform a risky surgery to lengthen my Achilles tendon, followed by six months in a wheelchair waiting to heal and hoping for the best. That didn't sound very hopeful to me.

One night, my mom took me to a faith-healing service. The evangelist prayed and I thought for sure I'd leave that service healed, but I walked back to the car in just as much pain as when I walked in.

That crooked walk was one of the reasons I became so hyper and adventurous. I knew the pain from the scoliosis could get worse with age, so I wanted to run, jump, swim, dance, and play as many sports as possible. Soon, I discovered that I could run better than I could walk. (Apparently, there are a lot of pigeon-toed athletes. Who knew?)

My best buddy, Chris, was the quarterback for our junior high football team, and I signed up to play wide receiver. The Walker Wolves were 6–0, setting up a high-stakes contest with our rivals, the Drakes of Blackduck High, who were also undefeated.

The showdown was held on the Drakes' home turf. It was Minnesota cold that night, our own little version of the Ice Bowl. We huddled up, blowing into our hands to try and stay warm.

It was a hard-fought game, with the score going back and forth between the Wolves and the Drakes. The game's final seconds ticked away, pausing with time for one final play. We were down by six points, twelve yards from a victory.

Chris snapped the ball. I juked left, then right. Suddenly, I was alone in the end zone, not a Drake defender in sight. The handful of Walker students and fans jumped to their feet, pointing to where I stood wide open. Chris faded back and lobbed a rainbow pass straight into my outstretched hands.

It ricocheted off my fingers. The bleachers gasped. It was like trying to catch a stick of butter. The ball slipped right through my hands, even though I'd caught that same pass ten thousand times from my dad in the yard. I guess the pressure got to me or something.

The football bounced in a sad little circle on the freshly mowed grass. My teammates fell to their knees, wailing, yanking off their helmets, and slamming them to the ground. A mighty cheer erupted from our opponents' bleachers. I stared at my throbbing hands, wondering why I'd even signed up for this torture. It's not like I was gonna get a college football scholarship or go on to play with the Minnesota Vikings someday.

I walked back to the sidelines, head down, knowing the mood in the locker room would be grim. In a small town, high school football is just behind Jesus in order of priority. *God help me, I just lost the big game. Hopefully, after the weekend, it won't be that big of a deal?*

I slipped into the school lobby the next Monday morning, trying to be low-key. After that game at Blackduck, people in gym class would yell out: "Blackduck 2008!" It wasn't just right after the game—it would go on for several years. People would say, "0-8," meaning 2008, and laugh, knowing I dropped the ball there.

Looking back, it all feels like some scene from a comedy. These days, Blackduck is one of my favorite memories from school, even the part where my classmates were laughing. There's something magical about laughter. It's hopeful. Sometimes, it can even be redemptive.

If you stay close to God, He'll help you turn trouble into something good. I wanted my classmates to laugh, but not because of some physical limitation or screwup I'd made. They'd be cracking up because I was the funniest, craziest kid in school.

.   .   .

I had been posting comedy videos to YouTube, and by the time I was in tenth grade they were starting to catch on. For one clip, I went to the rough part of Minneapolis to try and buy drugs. If they had anything, I'd whip out a fake badge and yell, "Freeze! Undercover cop!"

Instead of me chasing them, almost every time they'd realize I wasn't a real cop, and get mad that I punked them and chase me instead. It's crazy I didn't get shot. As I matured, I realized you didn't have to always cross the line to make something entertaining.

But doing comedy online at the time made me bolder at school. Walker High thought I was so hilarious that they recruited me and a friend to make our school's announcement videos. Joking around and acting wild made me popular with schoolmates, but most teachers found me annoying.

I'd have my whole class laughing, just going nuts. "Jimmy Kellogg!" the teacher would bark. "Settle *down!*" Then the intercom would crackle and say, "Teachers, turn on your TVs for an announcement." The screen would flicker, and my face would appear on the video, talking in a Jersey accent and cracking everybody up again.

My peers voted me class clown. I don't remember who came in second place, but I don't think it was even close.

. . .

A kid on Walker's student council got caught smoking weed, so they kicked him out and gave his spot to me. Later that year, the school took us to the statewide convention. At some point, the representative got on the microphone and asked, "Who here would like to run for president of all the student councils for our region?"

Four or five students raised their hands. *Why not?* I thought. I raised my hand too. My phone vibrated with a text from our teacher in charge, Mr. P.

Put your hand down. No more out of you or I'll write you up.

A short time later the convention stalled because of a mix-up in the speaking order. The adults in charge started shaking their heads, looking confused, handing papers back and forth. We were all watching and waiting. The teachers huddled up. Mr. P. walked over, only he wasn't mad this time. He looked embarrassed.

"There was a miscommunication and now we've got forty minutes with nothing to do," Mr. P. said. "Jimmy, we need you to go onstage and entertain all these kids."

Ha! It's all, *Be quiet, Jimmy,* when you've got business to do, but who do you call when everybody's bored and restless?

That's right, the class clown. I guess they didn't think I was completely useless.

I told some jokes and got everybody up to do the Harlem Shake (a *huge* viral trend back then). We had a dance-off and made a video. By then, I had graduated from my Flip Video to a GoPro Hero. A bunch of kids told me it was the best part of the day. Even the teachers were standing in the back of the room laughing. It was a hoot!

I felt like, for sure, that's what I was born to do. In less than one minute, I turned the atmosphere from boring and dreary to fun. Most teachers thought I was a nuisance, and looking back, I'm sure I made it hard for them to do their jobs sometimes. But I felt like the ability to bring people joy was a gift from God.

All I had to do was figure out what to do with my gift.

.   .   .

It was the voice that stopped me, a warm Southern drawl, humble but sure. My mom was watching TV from the kitchen. I'd just walked in the front door and couldn't see the screen.

"Hey, Mom, who is that?" I asked.

"Billy Graham," she said. "Your dad went to his crusade at the Metrodome right after he got saved."

I have a thing for voices and Billy Graham's reminded me of my grandfather's rich, smooth delivery. Authoritative but kind, always wise, patient, wanting the best for you.

I went upstairs to my room, closed the door, and looked up Billy Graham on YouTube. The first video listed was a short sermon called "Choices." I clicked on it and listened closely as Billy spoke about the power of priorities and how each of us makes a daily decision of who we will serve. He talked about sin and spiritual death, placing our hopes on the work of Christ alone.

Dr. Graham ended by saying, "Every secret thing will be brought out. But tonight, Jesus offers forgiveness. And more than forgiveness, He offers justification, just as though you had never committed a sin." Billy said the choice was urgent, that the longer you wait, the harder it becomes to decide.

"Are you going to live for yourself in this world?" Billy asked. "Or are you going to live for Christ?"

That message was preached over fifteen years before I was even born, but it felt like he was speaking directly to me. God showed up in my room that day. I knew what Billy Graham was telling me was the truth.

Like most kids who grew up in church, I would've told you that I believed in Jesus. But Billy Graham said even the demons believe in the existence of God and Jesus. Belief isn't enough. Every day, we make a choice to live for ourselves or God.

I didn't always make the right choices. Drinking and making out with strangers at parties, cussing. Not the *worst* behavior a teenager has ever committed—but not very good either.

Billy Graham said true faith changes what your life looks like. It changes your heart, your mind, and your appetites. I wanted to totally commit everything to God, but the truth is, I was afraid. So many Christians seemed to have boring lives, as if they started following Jesus and suddenly became half dead and downright depressed.

Still, I knew Billy was right. I had to make a choice. So, right there in my room, I got on my knees and prayed.

Please, Jesus, give me a crazy life. I'm all for being a committed Christian, but does being sold out to God mean you have to be safe and dull?

Moses' life was pretty crazy and the apostles were known for being a rowdy crew. The good kind of rowdy and crazy though. Joy over conformity, helping people over religious traditions, spontaneity over living uptight. I knew I wasn't capable of figuring out the balance between faith and relationship on my own. God would have to show me.

Soon enough, He would.

God Healed My Socks

They were all amazed, and they glorified God . . .
saying, "We have seen strange things today."

—LUKE 5:26 (KJ21)

One weekend, I went to a party in the forest with my high school friends. The location was a secret, but I made my way through the woods with the light from my phone. When I broke through to the clearing, I saw a big bonfire, pickup trucks backed up, tailgates down, kids sipping coolers with music booming.

We were messing around the fire, jumping around the flames, kicking it, and stuff like that. I was wearing a plain black T-shirt, shorts, and Vans with these socks my mom had bought me at Urban Outfitters that had Jesus on the sides. In a way, the Jesus socks were my testimony, a statement that I didn't need drugs or alcohol to have a good time. Watch me walk through the fire with Jesus on my feet.

After the bonfire, I came home and got undressed. My clothes smelled like smoke and my sock had a hole in it. Whether it was from the fire or from sticks in the woods, I'm not sure. I was terrified because my mom would know I'd been to a party, and the rip in the side would reveal it wasn't the youth group kind.

Jesus, I prayed, *please heal my socks.*

I peeled off my ruined socks and stuffed them in a drawer. Then I fell into bed and went to sleep.

The next morning, I woke up and got dressed. I opened the drawer and there lay the socks. No holes. No burns. No rips. Jesus on the side, arms stretched out, smiling.

I sat back on my bed, staring at the socks, retracing my steps, wondering if I could've dreamed it all somehow. *Did I have two pairs?* I looked again. I did not. *Was it possible my mom snuck in and replaced the burned socks?* Definitely not.

There was only one explanation: Jesus healed my socks.

I want to be your friend above anything else, a small voice said.

Chills went down my spine, and that's when it struck me. God was not mad at me, or the fun police, or some straitlaced religious figure that the church used to scare you into behaving. He cared about my life, and He was after my heart and was willing to do anything it took to get my attention—and this surely did. God didn't affirm my lifestyle and cover for me going to parties, but rather reached me how I needed to be reached at that time. And if God truly was that way, then there was nothing to fear; whatever might happen, Jesus wanted to be my friend.

I didn't know why God would heal a pair of socks while people were sick and starving. I still don't know. All I knew at that moment was that I had screwed up something too bad for me to fix. I needed God to help me. And sure enough, He did.

Are You Sure?

But in these last days he has spoken to us by his Son,
whom he appointed heir of all things, and through
whom also he made the universe.

—HEBREWS 1:2 (NIV)

"Jimmy, you believe what the Bible says, right?" Pastor Dainsberg asked.

Pastor Dainsberg was stoic and calm, the kind of manly man who'd use the cooking grease from Jimmy's Family Restaurant as bait when he went hunting for bear. We'd been attending his church ever since Pastor Rick moved to Florida. I wanted to do anything I could to grow in my faith, so I was excited when our preacher asked to meet with me.

"Yes, sir, I believe it," I assured him. "I really do." He nodded, measuring his reply while I checked out the wildlife mounted on the walls around his desk. "Well, Jimmy," he said, "I've been looking at your YouTube channel." Pastor Dainsberg leaned in, the look on his face stern but kind. "These videos you're making don't line up."

"Ohhh . . ."

It wasn't like I was hiding the videos. My parents had seen them. So had classmates and teachers at school. Sure, I might have been breakdancing in a blue Speedo, but it seemed like harmless fun. They knew I wasn't a bad kid.

Besides, my generation grew up on shows like *Fear Factor* and *Jacka***. You know that disclaimer they'd run before the show started?

WARNING:

DO NOT TRY THIS AT HOME

We were all trying those pranks and stunts at home.

My dad and his brother Danny were pranksters, and their teenage stories were as wild as mine. Probably wilder. My dad was the cameraman for many of my early videos, like the one on April Fools' where I'd go up to people on the street and say, "Hey! Why don't you kiss my . . ." and then I'd pull out a little stuffed donkey.

Some people threatened to kill me, but almost everybody laughed.

Pastor Dainsberg didn't think it was funny though. "Jimmy, if you really believe what you're saying, then you need to go home and delete those videos," he said.

That night, I sat in bed staring at my YouTube channel. I had built up nearly sixty videos with eighteen thousand followers and close to three million views. A million was still a huge number back then, but I had only made about four hundred and fifty dollars, and it probably cost me over ten thousand with all the videos I'd done.

Deleting those videos would be like throwing away my momentum, everything I had worked for in the last few years. Longer than that, ever since I'd started filming comedy clips when I was ten—before YouTube even existed! Erasing my videos felt like erasing myself.

I didn't want to go to college. I was already chasing my passion, hoping it'd turn into a career. Besides, I'd let my grades slip and couldn't get into a good school anyway. Making videos was my dream, but as I scrolled through thumbnail previews, I realized the message I'd been sending was mostly about impressing people and looking cool. My pastor had a point.

I started thinking about what the end of my life might look like. Old Man Jimmy would probably still want to be rocking the Speedo and jumping out of caskets for laughs. But seriously, as much as I loved comedians and pranksters, I knew I'd rather have one ounce of the conviction that Pastor Dainsberg and Billy Graham had. As I lay on my death bed, would I really be thinking *Dang, I wish I wouldn't have trusted God so much?*

With a deep breath, I selected all my videos and clicked on the little icon of a trash can.

>ARE YOU SURE? the pop-up cautioned.

I sat at the same desk where I had edited and uploaded all those videos, squiggling the mouse and circling my pointer over YES. The only thing I would ever regret is not surrendering everything to God. All my hopes and dreams and passions. All my work. The future and my past. Everything, all.

>ARE YOU SURE?

Oh dang, the devil's giving me one last chance to live for myself. When you choose to follow God, opposition will show up to try and make you doubt that choice.

I clicked YES. Just that fast, sixty videos, eighteen thousand followers, and three million views vanished. Forever.

. . .

I took a few days to clear my mind and listen to God. Editing raw footage and putting a story together—I was good at those things. Why would God want me to give up something I was naturally good at? Wouldn't that be a waste?

Videos weren't the problem. It was the content. All I needed to do was fine-tune my approach and start fresh.

I started thinking up new ways to hilariously surprise people and let them know that someone cared while ultimately pointing to God as our true source of wonder, laughter, and love. Giving away Bibles seemed like a good place to start, so I ordered several off Amazon and hid hundred-dollar bills inside the Book of John. Then I'd ride around at night searching for someone who looked like they needed encouragement.

You know who really needs a boost? Fast-food workers.

I knew what it was like to work in the restaurant business, but my family owned ours, and it wasn't fast food. Working at fast-food places can be tough. So, I started cruising through fast-food parking lots, my passenger seat full of Bibles with a hundred-dollar bill inside, praying, *Okay, God, who do You want me to help?*

One night, I saw this guy getting out of an old beater hatchback with a pizza delivery sign on top. There was pizza dough and sauce spilled all over his blue Domino's polo and he looked exhausted, like he'd just delivered forty-seven extra-large anchovy pizzas from Minnesota to Mexico.

I handed him the Bible. "What's this?" he said, confused.

"Open it," I replied, glad for once that it wasn't a prank.

I had the hundred-dollar bill bookmarking John 3:16. He saw the money and broke down crying and saying thanks. I figured that was God's way of showing me I was on the right track.

Oh, I still did crazy stunts too. Some Christians act like anything fun must be sinful, and I realized that a portion of that stereotype might have come from Christians in the Midwest. In that case, who better to change it than me?

I got ordained online for free—figuring it would be a lot quicker getting a certificate online rather than going through years of seminary school—and started baptizing people while wearing my Speedo and a big fur coat. In one of my first new videos, I baptized a close friend who weighed nearly three hundred pounds. I pinched his nose and dunked him underwater easily enough, but couldn't pull him back up. My friend nearly went straight from baptism to meeting Jesus in person.

For another video, I celebrated the Fourth of July weekend by putting on a Superman costume and parasailing over Leech Lake with a moldy parachute I'd found in a storage locker. Not only did my mom know that I was doing this stunt, but she was also the one driving the boat.

The parachute was kinda wet and sticky, and there were a bunch of pillars around the dock that I could've gotten tangled up in. It made for great footage though, and after, Philippians 4:13 popped up on the screen.

I CAN DO ALL THINGS THROUGH CHRIST WHO STRENGTHENS ME

The Bible says *all* things. Not just the boring stuff. Why couldn't "all things" mean making ridiculous videos that bring people closer to God?

Once Jesus healed my socks, everything broke open. That moment didn't feel like He was signing a blind waiver, agreeing to anything I wanted to try. It was more like a sign that God existed—and even thrived—outside of the box I had created for Him in my head.

I kept studying YouTube trends, trying to figure out that magic chemistry that makes a video pop. My edits got tighter, with more action and less filler—speedboats, Jet Ski jumps, and wipeouts thirty feet in the air.

Honestly, the videos were just as outrageous as before, but my objective had changed. How can I keep it clean while increasing views and engagement? How can I give more, share more, and talk about Jesus in a way that draws people in instead of pushing them away? How can I get better at my craft? Who should I partner with to take the work even further?

At the end of every video, I'd put an arrow saying "Click here to change your life," with a link to Billy Graham's "Choices" video. Then I'd pop up a Bible verse over some dubstep and end with a picture of Jesus DJing in space.

Now, maybe you don't think God is down with that kind of foolishness. That's okay. Check out this verse from 1 Corinthians: "I have become all things to all people so that by all possible means I might save some" (9:23, NIV).

The Life-Changing Power of Fun

*So I recommend having fun, because there is
nothing better for people in this world than
to eat, drink, and enjoy life.*

—ECCLESIASTES 8:15 (NLT)

Viewers seemed to enjoy the feel-good videos as much as I did. I wanted to bump the concept up a notch, so I grabbed a couple of friends and set out for Minneapolis, determined to find a stranger, take him for a day of fun, and capture it all on video. Sometimes, people underestimate the life-changing power of fun. Do you know what cuts through race, religion, culture, and age? Everybody likes to laugh and have a good time. Maybe I could be the apostle of fun?

We parked downtown and started walking. As I prayed for God to lead me to the right person, a vision flashed before me. Actually, not a vision. A real flash. As in Cordarrelle "Flash" Patterson, standing over by a city bus.

Cordarrelle was a wide receiver for the Minnesota Vikings—six foot two, two hundred and twenty pounds of solid muscle, with a wild tangle of braids sprouting from the top of his head. Flash still holds the NFL record for longest kick return at 109 yards. His record will never be broken. Do you know why? That's as far as you can go. There is no 110.

I ran over to him, camera recording. "Hey, Cordarrelle, you wanna go to the water park and then ride go-karts with me?" I asked.

Cordarrelle glanced over and shook his head. "No, man," he said.

"Okay!" I replied and kept walking. Nothing embarrasses me. A friend says that's my spiritual gift.

Soon, we saw this teenage guy coasting around on his bike. He looked sad, like maybe things hadn't been going his way, drifting slowly down the bike lane, like he needed to have a better day.

We talked and he told me his name was Nick. I showed him my YouTube channel and asked the same question I asked Flash Patterson, waterslides and all. Nick nodded and said, "Sure. I'm down."

First, we took Nick to Great Wolf Lodge, an indoor water park with go-karts and a bunch of other fun stuff. This rapper that I followed named Mike Stud was playing downtown at a famous nightclub called First Avenue, so

I figured we'd end the day at his show. I messaged Mike on Twitter from the go-kart track, saying that I was hanging out with this guy who was going through a hard time. Would it be okay if we came to the show?

Mike didn't respond. When you tweeted at someone on Twitter, it was public. Soon, all these other messages started pouring into his feed.

omg jimmy x mike collab would be crazzzzy
that would be awesome yall should totally work together
mike hook it up!!

The comments were from me. Most of them, at least. I had a good number of followers on Twitter at the time, but I also owned a few fake accounts just to hype things up. (Don't worry, that lesson's coming.)

Mike Stud saw all those messages and thought, *Wow, this kid's popping.* So, he messaged back. I told Mike that my goal was to find a down-and-out kid on the streets, give him the best day ever, and film the process.

Mike agreed. *Yeah, man, I'd love to help. Come on down.*

That night, Mike's crew waved us into the back before the show. We all took pictures together and Mike said he would call us up onstage during one of his songs. Before we left, he pulled me to the side. "Hey, Jimmy, me and my crew watched your videos and we really like your stuff," he said. "But we know you're crazy. Don't try to crowd-surf, okay?"

I nodded and thanked Mike. Nick, my two buddies, and I headed out front. A little while later, I got a text from Mike's manager.

Yo, Jimmy, come on up, do whatever you want, but DO NOT jump into the crowd. It's Mike's show. Don't steal the show. Plus, it's dangerous and we're liable if anybody gets hurt.

"Okay," I replied. "You got it."

First Avenue was jam-packed to see their hero that night and everybody was losing their minds. A few songs in, Mike invited me and Nick to the stage. I looked out over all those people, felt the adrenaline pumping, and thought, *Mike and his manager might've said no, but I bet when they see how dope this looks . . .*

"Okay, when I nod, we run and jump off the stage into the crowd," I told Nick. "Thing is, we both gotta jump or we're gonna be in big trouble."

I headed for the stage wearing nothing but a GoPro camera and my blue Speedo. Mike's manager met me at the steps and held his hand to my chest. "Nah, man, you can't be up here like that. Put your clothes back on."

I compromised and slipped back into my American flag pants and a shirt. Mike's manager rolled his eyes and waved us onstage. We were right out there with Mike Stud, dancing, hyping everybody up. The crowd was going crazy, singing along. I nodded to Nick. *Let's go!*

We ran to the edge of the stage. Just as we were about

to jump, Mike's song ended, the lights went out, and it was too late to stop.

BOOM!

I crashed into four people and we all hit the ground, laid out, moaning, checking for broken bones. The concert stopped. Three thousand people stared at me in silence. And then . . .

BOOOOOOOOOOO!

They started yelling and cursing, picking me up off the floor and pushing me back toward the stage. I looked for Nick, but he was already gone. "You suck, Darts!" someone in the balcony screamed.

Once I got up front, Mike Stud's security grabbed me, hauled me backstage, and started kicking the crap out of me. Finally, the club's bouncers pulled me away and threw me into the alley behind the club.

I lay there in a heap by the trash cans, shaking and scared. For all the pranks I'd pulled, I had never gotten punched or kicked. I'd never even been in a fight. But I knew all those Mike Stud fans were probably going to come looking for the tall, skinny guy who screwed up the show.

The Minnesota Twins were playing a few blocks over at Target Field, so I sprinted down and tried to blend into the safety of the crowd. My friends were still at First Avenue and we started texting.

How bad is it

                    where r u

ran to target field

                    ## STAY THERE

Eventually, I reached out to Mike. He said he was sorry his security guys beat me up and it was all good. If the story ended there, you could take it as a lesson about enthusiasm and making mistakes when you're trying to find your way. But that's not where the story ends.

Fast-forward a few years. I'm doing the kindness challenge and my videos are going viral. One day, I got a DM from Mike Stud on Instagram.

Man, I love what you're doing.

I messaged back. *Bro, you have no idea, but I'm the kid who tried to crowd surf at First Avenue and your crew beat the crap out of me.*

He didn't even remember that night. The only thing he said was *God's work, man.*

Mike and I even became friends. He likes and shares my content, and I've seen him regularly give back to people in his own way, which is inspiring to see. What if every small moment of connection—however outrageous—has the potential to start a chain reaction of generosity?

Still, it was stupid of me to jump in the crowd during

Mike's show. I could have hurt someone, and it wasn't right to steal his spotlight like that, especially after he'd been gracious enough to invite me and my new friend onstage. But the way all that came full circle? Right after I'd prayed for God to please give me a crazy life? No way that was just some coincidence. I had to be on the right track.

The Bible says all things work for the good of those who love the Lord. I don't get everything just right. I don't always think things through. God never asks us to get everything just right. The important thing is that we offer our lives, open to correction, walking in love, humility, and generosity. We might take a few punches along the way, but even our mistakes can be used for His glory.

If you step out on faith and ask God for a crazy life, you might end up with a collection of crazy stories, some that make you smile and others that make you wish you could go back and make a better choice. But when I look back on all those cool, crazy stories, I see the hand of God in every step, how patient He's been with me, how He works things out for the good.

Maybe you're reading this and thinking you've made too many mistakes. Maybe you're thinking about how those mistakes have made a mess out of your life and now you're stuck and don't know what to do next. If we walk in love and simple trust, our worst stories and biggest mistakes can be redeemed.

A preacher at school used to tell us, "If it's not good, it's not the end, because God turns all things to good for those that love Him."

The key in that is *for those that love Him.* You can't be living in sin, have a wicked heart, do horrible things, and expect good things to come out of that. But if you have a heart of repentance from the actual wrongdoings and you see what happened, He can turn those messes and mistakes we've made into something beautiful. That's pretty fire.

Town Fool

But God has chosen the foolish things of the world to put to
shame the wise, and God has chosen the weak things of the
world to put to shame the things which are mighty.

—1 CORINTHIANS 1:27

In my senior year, Walker High organized a trip to Minneapolis for WE Day, a massive youth empowerment festival held in major cities nationwide. WE Day featured
celebrity speakers and anti-bullying messages for students
in a leadership program called Interact.

I was a member of Interact and known for my You-
Tube skills, so the sponsors from school asked me to
document the trip. They even bought me some new
equipment so I could step up the production value.

We piled on a bus and headed to WE Day Minneapolis. The Xcel Energy Center was packed to the rafters
with about twenty thousand teens. The Jonas Brothers were there, as were Demi Lovato, Martin Luther
King III, players from the Minnesota Vikings, and Nick

Vujicic, the Christian motivational speaker with no arms or legs.

I was sitting in the upper level with my class, filming. My cousin Grant texted.

you're at that we day thing?

yeah

bro you gotta take advantage
of that

I looked around at the purple spotlights swirling over a sea of teens, every face focused on a giant stage surrounded by screens. Thousands of kids, captive. I texted Grant back.

you're right

I handed my camera to a classmate. "Just film the stage, okay?" I said.

Our Spanish teacher was in charge, so I leaned down and shouted into her ear when I passed. "Hey, I'm gonna run down and give a quick speech, okay?"

"Yeah, right," she replied sarcastically. "Sounds good."

That little bit of leeway was all I needed. Technically, I had permission, so . . .

I made my way to the first tier of security. "Whoa, whoa," the guard said, holding up a hand to stop me. "Where do you think you're going?"

I was wearing a plain black T-shirt, just like the television crew. "I'm an intern for CBS," I told them. "I need to get to my crew."

The first line of security waved me through and I raced down to floor level, about fifty yards from the stage. I tried the CBS intern thing, but the huge guy blocking my way shook his head. "You don't have the right credentials," he said, pointing toward the exit. "I'm gonna need you to head back that way."

"I'm shooting a video for our school project and I *really* need this one shot." I pressed my hands together and made a desperate face. "It won't take a second. *Please?*"

"All right," Security Guy sighed. "One quick shot and you're out."

I moved closer, phone up, pretending to film. A ruckus stirred in the lower deck. The security guard whipped around to check it out. As soon as he turned, I darted in close and crouched low.

Minnesota's most famous news anchors were onstage, getting everybody pumped up. The entire area was surrounded by guards. *Even if I make it up there, I'm gonna get tackled and tased before I can say a word on the mic,* I thought.

Then I remembered the key to pulling pranks, like I'd done in all those videos. Confidence. You can't hesitate or act like a sneak. You gotta own it.

I stood, walked onto the platform past security, and

marched straight up to ace anchorman Frank Vascellaro, who was holding the microphone. "Excuse me, sir, can I say something?"

Frank shot me a confused look, like maybe he missed his cue. Then he handed me a hot mic, and I was standing in the spotlight with my face on a forty-foot screen behind me, flanked by even bigger jumbotrons on both sides.

Thousands of kids stared back, waiting to hear what I had to say. But I didn't have anything planned. So, I had to wing it.

"What's up, everybody! I'm Jimmy Kellogg and I want to change this country for the better. If someone's telling you that you can't do something, run them over like a speed bump! You can do *anything*. I'm from a big, tall, small town called Walker, Minnesota, and I put out videos on YouTube every week! Shout-out to my Lord and Savior, Jesus Christ, baby!"

Even though I kinda biffed it, the crowd exploded with cheers. I held up the peace sign and returned the mic to cohost Frank.

"Wow!" he said, realizing I wasn't a scheduled speaker. "Story of the *week*!"

I walked down the steps back to floor level. As I made my way through the crowd, people's hands stretched out to offer me high fives. *So far, so good.*

Security surrounded me as soon as I walked into the outer hall. A short, stout woman stepped in close. Two walkie-talkies, all-access laminate. A badge let me know she was the boss.

"I have to get you in trouble because that's my job," she said. Then she leaned in and whispered, "But I just want you to know, I love what you said up there."

The security team led me to a holding room. My heart started beating so hard and fast it felt like a rave in my chest. Then they brought my Spanish teacher in. "Señor Jimmy," she said, "you are in big trouble."

First, I had to call my principal and tell her what I had done. As I was confessing, my phone began to blow up. The teens in the arena started following me, and once the video of my speech hit socials, thousands of new followers joined in, some of them messaging me and reaching out.

The other kids bully me at school, what should I do?

I'm pregnant. How do I tell my parents?

Jimmy, help, bro, I'm feeling suicidal and don't know what to do . . .

Ding, ding, ding, notifications of new subscribers, messages popping up. I guess they thought I was a motivational speaker, like the others who'd spoken that day.

I ended up having to write a bunch of apology letters

to the school, the news stations, and the WE Day team. My school banned me from all future field trips. I wasn't allowed at any school event that had a microphone. And, of course, I got suspended.

When I walked back into Walker High three days later, my classmates started chanting my name. Everybody had seen that video. "You put our town on the map, Jimmy!" one kid said.

I started helping those who reached out to me online and at my school. Everyone was looking at me like some super-supportive voice of inspiration, so I took on that role, listening to their stories and telling them how much encouragement I'd gotten from my faith. Even a few of my teachers pulled me aside and told me they admired what I was doing.

"Jimmy," one teacher said, "you'll probably either end up famous or in jail. Maybe both."

I did not win class clown that year. Oh, my classmates voted for me, but after that stunt I pulled at WE Day, my school changed the title from Class Clown to Town Fool. Yep, just for me.

Ha! Kinda dirty, but I got a kick out of it. Sounds a lot bigger that way.

WE Day jump-started my social media career and gave me a platform to speak to my peers. I don't know why they responded so positively to what I said onstage that day. Maybe it was the surprise of it all, that some random kid—just like them—had been able to slip on-stage at this huge event and pull it off. Maybe it's because my speech wasn't practiced or planned. It may not have been profound, but at least it was real.

Life to the Fullest

In the end, it's not about the stunts or the pranks but the
friendships and memories you make along the way.

—PHILIP J. CLAPP,
AKA JOHNNY KNOXVILLE

In the spring of my senior year, reports started pinging all
over my social media feeds promising that the city of
Ames, Iowa, was popping and 2014 just might be the
craziest VEISHEA ever.

VEISHEA was a massive weeklong celebration held
on the campus of Iowa State, so big that even John Wayne,
Ronald Reagan, and the Black Eyed Peas showed up.
(Not all together, I don't think, but VEISHEA was so
outrageous that you never know.) The festival had already
been shut down after riots in 1988, '92, '94, and 2004, so
when they said VEISHEA 2014 might be even wilder, I
knew I had to go.

I strapped on my GoPro and headed straight for Iowa
State's campus to start filming content. As soon as I parked

and got out, it was obvious the reports were true—and then some! The air was charged with electricity, students flipping cars over and knocking down light poles, fire alarms screaming, breaking glass. I stripped down to my Speedo, scribbled all over my face with a Sharpie, and ran straight into the madness.

Chaos is better than Disneyland to me. That thrill when nobody knows what will happen next and everyone is caught up in the moment, laughing, wild, and alive. You're probably saying, "Hang on, Jimmy, didn't you just delete all those outrageous videos after meeting with your pastor a few chapters back?" Yeah, but I thought it was all good because I was showing everybody that you didn't need drugs or alcohol to have a good time. The method might seem unconventional, but I really was trying to point people toward God. Since Jesus healed my socks at a party, I thought that perhaps I was called to minister to frat row.

Besides, I was already a regular at campus parties. My YouTube channel had become so popular, students would hit me up to come and make videos where I stirred everybody into a frenzy, hosting contests to see which university could be the most extreme. When I showed up, you never knew what would happen next. Running across tables in a busy restaurant, busting through doors and breakdancing with old ladies, smacking myself until my nose bled, messing with the police. I knew I'd never get in trouble, because I was sober. What could they charge me with?

Unless you grab people's attention, you won't succeed on social media. One of my most popular clips showed me falling asleep in a busy intersection, backing up traffic for miles. Some people thought they were going to be late for work, so they got mad and dragged me out of the road.

"Ohh, sorry," I claimed groggily. "I've been having a tough time with this narcolepsy."

Check this out—my dad was the one filming me! When he saw the cops coming, he pulled me to the side. "Hurry, switch shirts with me," he said. "That way, you won't match their description."

We swapped quickly, but then my mom called and said there were cops at the hotel looking for me, so we couldn't go there. They ended up catching me at a restaurant later on.

Maybe you could argue the theology of whether stuff like that was wrong or right. What you can't argue with is this: that was one of the coolest, most fun days my dad and I ever had. I just called him on speaker so we could laugh and tell that story again.

I'm not saying all of this to boast about bad behavior or suggest God was giving me a big thumbs-up for hassling people and causing traffic jams. But there's something about adventure that brings people together.

Viral videos and social media success could end tomorrow. You know what I'll have forever? Great stories. I mean, what stories would make it into your book? The crazy ones, right?

You don't have to become some boring straitlaced clone to follow God. Lean into what makes you different and trust that you'll find guidance along the way. For me, the goal was (and is) to be extravagant, bold, and in the moment while maintaining a pure heart.

Purpose is not a straight shot. You're going to make mistakes. When you miss the mark, it's an opportunity to learn, grow, and seek God again.

.   .   .

Walker High School was buzzing with rumors about what kind of grand finale stunt I had planned for graduation. I stayed quiet until graduation morning, when I posted this update online.

I've done some crazy things in my life, but nothing compares to tonight . . .

Walker High lost their minds. Teachers, coaches, the principal. Pastor Dainsberg called my dad. Even my classmates were certain that I was going to create the sort of mayhem that could spoil our ceremony.

That night, Walker High hired a couple of off-duty police officers to keep an eye on me. I'd walk by and talk into my collar like there was a hidden mic, mumbling things like, "Yeah, yeah, it's still on. These guys are rookies."

My buddies who came to watch got a pat-down and stern lecture about the significance of graduation and how it should be respected and taken seriously. As our marching band played "Pomp and Circumstance," the senior class of 2014 filed into the gym and sat on folding chairs.

You know that feeling like you're being watched? It wasn't a feeling. The whole place was tense. It felt like every eyeball was glaring at me and waiting for whatever chaos I'd prepared to begin.

And waiting. And waiting . . .

The big stunt was . . . there was no stunt. I didn't have anything planned. I just wanted to stir up my small town and get them wondering and gossiping about what kind of nonsense I'd try. The things they imagined were better than anything I could have come up with.

Our commencement speaker told us to believe in ourselves and the valedictorian did too. The Walker High band played a slow song from some movie before we marched up to get a fancy piece of paper that said we were done with high school.

Then something did happen. Something completely unplanned.

Remember when I said I would smack myself to stir up a crowd? It was really just a party trick because my nose would bleed so easily. Often blood would start pouring out of my nose for no reason at all. Like on graduation night in the gym.

It was only a trickle at first. I wiped it on my sleeve and tilted my head back, staring at the cobwebs caked around the gymnasium lights.

Tipping my head back usually made the bleeding stop. Not on that night. Pretty soon, it was a gusher, dripping onto the shiny gym floor.

The school staff and cops were ready, leaning forward like, *here we go*. They called for my row to stand. I stuck a Kleenex to my nose, walked up, got my diploma, and sat back down.

You know what's weird? I think everybody was disappointed. Even the police and our principal. Sometimes, the best prank is to just keep them guessing.

Except nobody would have guessed this: Ten years later, Walker High asked me to come back and speak. Who would've ever predicted that twist?

Maybe God likes pulling pranks too.

·   ·   ·

There are plenty of people who will tell you all the things you cannot do. Don't listen to them. The dream was put in you for a reason. Go for it. You can do *anything*. Even if you don't achieve your dream, you'll have the peace of knowing you tried.

I didn't say it quite that articulately at WE Day, but that's the message I wanted to share with others. Adults might miss it or forget, but the kids know what's real. That's straight out of the Bible, by the way. If you really want to find God's plan and God's way, you gotta approach life like a little kid.

So, don't ever stop being a kid. Don't ever get so jaded that you stop believing in dreams. Belief will take you further than talent ever could.

III

What's Cookin'

Undeniable Touch

Put your dreams on the altar.
They will be resurrected into something even grander.

—LOREN CUNNINGHAM

After my sister Chelsie graduated high school, she applied to Youth with a Mission's Discipleship Training School in Australia. Youth with a Mission (YWAM) trains young people for Christian missions through classes in Bible study and evangelism. Chelsie was accepted to the program, and our entire family took her over when I was fifteen.

Once Chelsie completed her training, YWAM sent her to India and she came back with all these incredible stories of the sick being miraculously healed.

Chelsie came back so on fire for the Lord that I was like, *Holy buckets! Maybe I ought to do that someday.*

Fast-forward: After finishing high school, I was trying to figure out what God wanted me to do next. YWAM had a program in Kona, Hawaii—why not? I could shoot some sick videos there and help people out when the camera wasn't rolling.

Then I watched a YouTube clip about the missionary work YWAM was doing worldwide. It broke my heart and made me want to help people even more. Sure, I'd deleted my old prank videos and made a change, but surrendering my life to Jesus in my bedroom had only been the beginning. I needed to encounter God deeper and more powerfully. To do that, I knew I would have to leave Minnesota.

Once I landed in Hawaii, I started having second thoughts. This wasn't some luxury resort on the ocean. YWAM was a primer for world missions: everybody stacked into bunk beds, sweltering humidity and no AC, three-inch flying cockroaches, stinging centipedes, and tiny fire ants in your food and clothes.

What have I gotten myself into?

For the first few days, I reverted to that shy, anxious kid—out of my element, unsure. Eventually, I made a few friends and got a chance to look around town. Kona is dope and their coffee was seriously delicious. Our campus was about a half mile from the bay. Right behind us, there was a Walmart, Taco Bell, tire store, 7-Eleven—all the regular town stuff.

One day while exploring I met a homeless man named

Freddie. He had a big gray beard that flowed down past his chest and was just the chillest cat ever. It's hard to be homeless anywhere, but if I had to pick between the beaches of the Big Island and the cold, hard streets of Minneapolis? I'd be a little more chill in Hawaii too.

I took Freddie for ice cream and to the Regal Maka-lapua to see *Big Hero 6,* the animated Disney movie about a giant snowman-looking robot. Neither of us realized it was in 3D.

"What the heck?" I said about fifteen minutes in. "Why's everything all fuzzy?"

"Man, don't ask me," Freddie said. "I ain't been to a movie in twenty years. I thought maybe it was supposed to look that way."

We both walked out with headaches, laughing. Right next to the theater door was a bucket of 3D glasses with the *Big Hero 6* logo on the side. "Ohh, baby," I said, picking up a pair and putting them on. "Were we supposed to wear these, you think?"

"Jimmy, you're crazy, man," Freddie said, cracking up again.

YWAM had a big focus on street outreach, where we went out into the community telling people about God, but I believed ministry could be just hanging out with someone from the streets and being their friend. In a way,

Freddie and I ministered to each other. I was feeling pretty homesick before that day, but Freddie was a blast. He reminded me why I was there.

.   .   .

We were gathered under a massive white canvas tent for story night, listening to the previous YWAM class testify about the miracles they had experienced out in the field. After the testimonies, we watched *Holy Ghost,* a documentary about the global outpouring of signs and wonders. Sage was our team leader, a clean-cut guy in his late twenties, seriously mission-minded and filled with the Spirit. I was sitting in this little plastic chair watching the film when he walked over and quietly said, "Jimmy, do you need healing?"

"Yeah, bro," I replied. "I've had terrible scoliosis all my life. My left leg is shorter than the right one and I'm pretty much in pain all of the time."

Sage looked straight into me. "Do you want to get healed?"

Crazy question, huh? Then I thought about when Jesus asked that crippled guy by the pool the same thing. I looked at Sage and nodded. "Sure," I told him. "Go for it."

Sage kneeled beside me, taking my legs in his hands. "In Jesus' name," he prayed, "grow."

No way I was closing my eyes for that prayer. I wanted to watch. For the first few seconds, nothing happened. Suddenly, my leg began to shake violently, extending, shifting my hips, pulling my back straight, like an electrical current shooting up to my neck. *Whoa!* I stood, testing one leg and then the other, walking from the tent and out into the street. Walking, running, jumping, going nuts.

All my life, I'd lived with constant pain, like a knife in my back, whenever I drove or tried to be active. Stabbing and burning me when I tried to sleep or if I sat in one place for too long. Seeing a pair of socks get healed is one thing, but now I had just watched my leg grow out. And the pain was gone.

It was like a giant neon sign on the moon that said GOD IS REAL! I was thankful and shaking and scared, but I knew I couldn't have my own version of Christianity where I could party and be a Christian too. It created a fear of God, which is the beginning of all wisdom. It wasn't "be a Christian" to have good morals and tradition but because God was real and there was no hiding from Him. One day we're going to stand before Him and give account of our life.

This was more than an opinion or theology or an emotional response. I'd experienced an undeniable touch from God. Whatever it took, I wanted to share that experience with others.

Miracles Beneath the Mount Everest of Trash

All things are possible to him who believes, less difficult to him who hopes, easy to him who loves, and still easier to him who perseveres in the practice of these three virtues.

—BROTHER LAWRENCE

"Oh, snap," I told my teammates. "Look at that giant mountain."

Its peak filled the sky as the Youth with a Mission van rumbled toward India's capital city, thick gray clouds drifting across the summit. I flicked on my camera and rolled down the window to document the beginning of our trip. That's when the stench hit.

"Ugh," Julie said. *"Jimmy."*

Julie, Elise, Kyle, and I were the eager teens sent forth to minister to the lost and hurting in New Delhi. As our van drew closer, I could see that the mountain was not a mountain. At least not one made of stone. It was a pile of garbage, and the clouds were just pollution.

Dead cows and bright yellow plastic bags, billions of bottles, food wrappers, and broken glass formed a man-made Mount Everest of trash with vultures circling and children scampering around. These were little kids, too, like a three-year-old leading a two-year-old by the hand to poke through the garbage with a stick.

"Breathing the air here is like smoking two packs of cigarettes a day," our team leader, Sage, told us as I hurried to roll the window up. "See all those black spots on top? It even kills the birds."

We made our way into town. A local Christian family had agreed to let us stay in their home. Kyle and I slept in the lower level while Elise and Julie took the nicer room upstairs. After the long trip in, I was ready to shower and get some rest. This was the shower: you filled a metal bucket with water and poured it over your head. "Whatever you do," our host warned, "don't get any in your mouth."

I was doing some push-ups before bed and a big, hairy rat ran under me. Then a mighty racket pierced the walls and it sounded like somebody's grandpa getting hooked to jumper cables while holding a box of keys. I peeked outside. Some guy in a long robe was chanting and banging a stick covered in bells.

"Oh, that's just the Nightwatcher," our host explained. "He walks the streets at night to ward off evil spirits."

"All night?" I asked.

Our host just smiled.

The next morning, Sage came over to give us the day's mission: A man in the village named Sing-Pi had been a successful engineer before getting mixed up in witchcraft. Since then, he'd spent most of the last five months hiding under a blanket and lashing out violently at times.

The four of us piled into a tuk-tuk (a tiny three-wheeled taxi) and headed deeper into the city. People were everywhere, crowded around food carts and open-air markets, worshipping different statues of their gods. (There are thirty-three million gods in the Hindu belief.)

Twenty minutes later, we arrived at Sing-Pi's. His family told us he was on the roof. Houses there have flat roofs, like in the Bible. "Can I use your bathroom?" I asked.

This woman handed me a long stick and pointed to the alley. I checked the end of the stick, thinking it might have a key attached, like at the gas station. Nope. Turns out the bathroom was a hole in the ground and a chair with the seat cut out. Pigs will attack you while you're trying to do your business, so you gotta use the stick to drive them back.

After the fastest bathroom break in India's history, I joined my teammates on the roof. Sing-Pi was lying in the corner with a blanket over his head. We pulled the blanket off and helped him sit up. His eyes were solid white and lifeless, thick black hair in wild swirls, flies swarming around his face.

"Let's just try to clean him up and love on him the best that we can," Julie said.

She filled a pan with water and we washed Sing-Pi's feet, praying and telling him that whatever happened, he could be well and whole again. A single tear rolled down his cheek as we promised that God still loved him.

We trimmed Sing-Pi's hair and dressed him in a clean shirt before leading him downstairs and into the town center. Julie bought him a cup of chai, but when we tipped Sing-Pi's head back to help him drink, the tea ran down the corners of his mouth onto his shirt. The four of us were sitting on a bench, trying to figure out what to do next. An older man with a cane shuffled past, his eyes milky gray.

"Hello, sir?" I said. We talked with the help of our local team translator and it turned out the old man was blind. After I had my back healed, I took the Bible at face value, and when it said "Lay your hands on the sick and they will recover," I believed it. "Can I pray for you?" I asked.

He nodded and I laid my hand on his shoulder. "Eyes be healed, in Jesus' name."

The old man flinched back. "Pray again!" he pleaded. "In the name of Jesus, *be healed.*"

He jerked his head around, first left, then right. "Again! Again!" the old man said, waving his hands.

At first, he could see shadows. I prayed some more and he could start to see light. I kept praying until eventually, the old man turned and ran away.

"Hey, wait!" I called, wanting to hear his story, hoping a good testimony would encourage our group. With a shrug, I walked back over to my teammates. Sing-Pi was slumped against the bench rail, no better than before.

Ten minutes later, the blind man returned. But he wasn't blind anymore. His eyes were clear and he had run to tell the whole village how he'd been healed. They came back with him to see the crazy Americans for themselves.

If I have any strength, it's childlike faith. God moves through me most when I'm like a kindergartner in the Garden of Eden.

"Jesus wants to heal you too!" I told them.

All four of us began to lay hands on people as fast as we could. Healings broke loose every few seconds, deaf ears opening and broken limbs going straight. Children rushed to us, pulling at our clothes.

The crowd grew so large that we could not reach them all. "Just so you know, there's nothing special about us," I shouted. "You can lay your hand on the person next to you and pray in the name of Jesus."

People started praying for one another and God's healing power spread like a fire. Headaches vanished, shoulders popped back into place, broken bones became straight again.

Elise and Julie were laying hands on a man with paralyzed feet. His friends had carried him nearly two miles to find us. They didn't have to carry him back. He walked home, completely healed.

A group of elders showed up, angry that we were speaking the name of Jesus. They started cursing us. Somebody threw a brick. It felt like a riot was about to break loose, and not the VEISHEA kind.

"We need to go," Kyle suggested. Everybody agreed. Besides, we'd been out for hours, and it was beginning to get dark. I looked back at the bench. Sing-Pi was still there, surrounded by flies, fists clenched, oblivious to everything that had taken place.

Some of the crowd followed as we walked him back. Doors opened on the way, villagers begging for help with their sick. By the time we returned, it was night. We led Sing-Pi to the roof and sat him beside his blanket.

God had moved. Hundreds had just been healed. So why was Sing-Pi no better than before?

Sage came to join us on the roof. He was the one who

prayed when my back got healed, so I was looking to him for our next move. But Sage just looked back at me.

"Well, Jimmy, go for it," he said casually. "Cast it out."

I knew the Bible talked about Jesus casting out demons, but I wasn't sure where those verses were, so I opened it to a random spot near the middle and started to read.

"Your breasts are like two fawns, twins of a gazelle."

Sing-Pi growled. I closed the Bible and he stopped. Flipping a few pages over, I read again. "The curves of your thighs are like jewels."

"GrrRRRRR!" Sing-Pi dug his nails into my wrist at the reading of the Word. Was this the Word? I checked the cover to make sure. *Dang!* I thought. *The Old Testament is wild.*

Kyle and Sage were praying while Elise and Julie sang about the joy of the Lord. I turned from the risqué parts of the Bible over to Genesis. "In the beginning God created the heavens and the earth . . ."

Sing-Pi snarled and spit, but I was determined not to quit this time. I was reading about God dividing light from the darkness when everything got quiet, from chaos to total peace.

"Jimmy, look," Julie said. "It left him. He's free."

When I looked up, Sing-Pi was sitting quietly. The flies were gone and his eyes were no longer white and lifeless. At first, he was confused. Then his family rushed in and threw their arms around him, and he broke down.

Sing-Pi heard us say thousands of words all day and his eyes remained closed. But as soon as we read God's Word, his body and spirit reacted. He didn't speak English and I didn't know up from down on the mission field, but when I read the Word, a demon left his body. Those words had power.

Later, I found the verses about Jesus and demons, over twenty-five of them through Matthew, Mark, Luke, and John. Jesus cast seven devils out of Mary Magdalene, and she still got to be the first person in history to preach the Good News. You don't have to do everything exactly right. The Bible says we can perform miracles like Jesus if we only trust and believe. In fact, John 14:12 says we will do even greater things. Of course, there are people all around the world that can fake miracles and do it for the wrong reasons or for themselves. You never want to throw the baby out with the bathwater when God calls us in Scripture to pray and watch what He will do. There's nothing more powerful than a genuine and sincere prayer knowing that you're not doing it, but it's God wanting to touch someone through you.

It was quite a scene up on that rooftop. Everybody hugged and cried and we stood there feeling like the love of God was bigger than any sickness or evil spirit or mountain made of trash. Jesus healed hundreds that day, but He never forgot about that one lost sheep. Neither did we. We kept on believing until Sing-Pi came home.

Here's the best part: It wasn't a one-day thing. The miracles continued the entire three months we were in India. I could fill another entire book just with the incredible things that happened on that trip. That day, we saw firsthand with Sing-Pi that God leaves the ninety-nine for the one, and that's how I wanted to live my life.

Flushing Hell

You must not make for yourself an idol of any kind or an
image of anything in the heavens or on the earth or in the
sea. You must not bow down to them or worship them,
for I, the LORD your God, am a jealous God who will
not tolerate your affection for any other gods.

—EXODUS 20:4–5 (NLT)

"I would give up everything for Jesus," I boasted to my
roommates.

After our mission trip to India, I went to the Sunshine
Coast region of Australia for a nine-month intensive
Bible study program that was supposed to be "the equiv-
alent of sixty years in church." They put me in a house
with five other Bible school guys. Sometimes, young
Bible school students like to brag about who's the most
on fire for the Lord.

"What about your videos?" my housemate shot back.
"Would you give Jesus that?"

"What do you mean?" I'd already given up the crazier
videos, anything with cussing or dirty pranks.

"Yeah, but your subscribers came over from watching the old stuff," he said. "So, those were gained through sin."

I was like, *Aw, man, here we go again. Anytime you have money saved, you gotta give it all away. Anytime you're good at something, you have to quit. If every Christian that's good at something has to give it up through a false sense of humility, how can the Kingdom of God ever truly advance?*

Still, I couldn't stop thinking about his question. I did talk about my online work a lot—but seriously? If Jesus and the Bible are in all my videos, how could that be sinful?

Not long after, I shot a video at the area's biggest toy store, buying local kids a thousand dollars' worth of presents. Australia's news channel did a feature story, and they put it on the front page of their newspaper, *The Courier-Mail.*

The newspaper even mentioned my previous trip to the region. "At one stage, Darts caused traffic chaos when he pretended to be sleeping in the road in Mooloolaba, near Oceans resort." Yep, that's where my dad and I almost got arrested filming a stunt four years earlier.

Right below our feature was an article about a sewage problem titled "Flushing Hell." The way they positioned the headline made it look like we were flushing hell by handing out toys. What are the chances? It was like a wink from God.

Crazy paradox. My Bible study mate was saying I should give up making videos while the fruit of those videos was being celebrated on the news, little kids laughing and screaming, spreading joy and hope. I'd told the reporters about Jesus, how He'd changed my life since I pranked the cops down under, and the importance of sharing God's love through example rather than lecturing or shoving it down people's throats.

I kept posting new videos from Australia but couldn't stop thinking about my roommate's challenge. *Are videos really still an idol to me?*

One night I couldn't sleep, so I picked up my Bible and took a deep dive into what Scripture had to say.

"Those who cling to worthless idols forfeit the grace that could be theirs" (see Jonah 2:8).

"All who make idols are nothing. The things they treasure are worthless" (see Isaiah 44:9).

The Bible doesn't just call us to give up the sinful things. It says we have to drop anything that could get in the way of God. An idol doesn't always mean some wicked-looking statue on a platform. It's whatever we elevate to a higher position than God. Even religion can become an idol for some.

I went back and forth, from posting new videos to feeling the heat of conviction and making them all private so no one else could see. Friends would notice and say things like "Why would you stop? Your videos help people. You're doing a good thing." I even had my cousin offer to buy the channel from me if I stopped because he thought it would be crazy if I just threw it away.

.   .   .

I had two months of Bible school left and it was like serving time at Rikers Island. YWAM had been three months. India had been another three months. Nine months in one place? It felt like nine years to me.

I had a roommate named Norway Eddie. Norway Eddie had these wild, fiery eyes, as if he really did sneak away to meet face-to-face with God. There was such an incredible sense of peace about him that one day I had to ask, "Eddie, what is it about you that's so different?"

"Do you want to know the secret to Christianity?" he replied.

"Yeah! What is it?"

Norway Eddie leaned in. "The Secret Place," he said, eyes on fire. "It's where Jesus is and that's the secret to Christianity."

Quiet time is difficult when you have five roommates, but we had this ugly little shed behind our house where I would go to pray. It was so small I could barely stand up, and spiders were skittering everywhere. I hate that stuff. I had a pretty good chance of meeting Jesus in that shed because half of the spiders in Australia have enough venom to send you to heaven. But if I could find God's presence, it would be worth it.

Every afternoon, I would walk out to the shed, headphones on, praying out loud and singing my face off to songs like "Never Going Back" and "Simple Gospel," trying to find the secret place where Jesus lives.

One day, my mind was still and everything else in the world felt far away. Instagram feeds and YouTube view counts, roommates, and Bible schools. I was lifted above that tiny shed to a place where there were no more words to sing or pray. Time stopped. It felt like I could float up through that tin roof and never come back down.

A hand rested on my shoulder. I jumped and spun around, expecting to see one of my roommates standing there. The shed was empty.

It's like God was saying, *Hey, it's Me, Jimmy. I'm here. You might never feel My touch or sense My presence in this way again. But I'm here with you. Always.*

What can you say after an experience like that?

Whoa.

If I'd come halfway around the world for that one moment, it was worth every mile. I didn't ever want to let anything get between me and God. I wanted to meet with Him like that until someday I lifted up through the sky and never came back down again.

.   .   .

The program in Australia finally ended. I was home in Minnesota, back in the room where my socks got healed, where I surrendered my life to God after watching Billy Graham. The same room where I posted the first video I ever made.

I was still wrestling with making videos. Was I clinging to an idol? Was I guilty of finding value and self-worth through my online presence rather than a relationship with the Lord? I did not want to forfeit grace. I did not want ever to lose access to the secret place.

I deleted everything. Facebook, Twitter, Instagram, YouTube—gone. Whatever validation, purpose, or job skills I was getting from views and making videos I needed to get from God.

Erasing my videos was like going through drug withdrawal. I sat in my room staring out over Leech Lake, feeling like I didn't exist. Anxiety whipped me like a storm over the water. I'd reach to check my phone and see how the feeds were doing. *Oh, yeah. There's nothing to check.* Some sick new idea for a video would pop into my head and I'd feel that rush of excitement—until I remembered there were no more videos.

Nobody knew what I was doing and I couldn't check in on friends without making the effort to reach out directly. Living disconnected in a digital age felt crazy, especially since it was the only thing I'd ever known. But after a few weeks away from social media, something shifted. I experienced more joy, more pleasure, and a deeper intimacy with God than ever before. It felt like I had an audience of a billion people, but it was only God. His presence gave me more satisfaction than all the attention in the world could ever give.

After a few weeks, things began to settle down. My mind was getting clearer and less distracted. In the empty spaces, I spent more quiet time with the Lord. Except really *with* God and not just half listening to Jesus while scrolling through stuff on my phone.

Keep Austin Weird

Don't settle for a normal life. Not when you can enjoy the wonderful weirdness of being who God created you to be.

—CRAIG GROESCHEL

I was driving across the prairie on my way to Austin, Texas. In the middle of nowhere, I saw a tiny guy hitch-hiking under the ruthless Texas sun. I kept driving, checking my rearview mirror.

I can't pass this guy up. He'll be buzzard food.

It was a one-way section of interstate, so I had to slam my Honda in reverse and backtrack for about a hundred yards until I pulled up beside him. This poor guy was about four foot nine and ninety pounds, so I wasn't too worried he'd carjack me or try anything bad.

"Come on in," I said, reaching across to open the door. "My name's Jimmy."

He flopped down in the seat like a man receiving a last-minute pardon from death row. "Juan," he replied woozily.

Juan told me he was on his way to help his son when the police impounded his car, so he had to walk back home to San Antonio. His lips were all cracked and he wasn't even sweating. That's when I realized he'd probably been walking through the Texas heat for a long time.

Hold up, right? You're wondering why I was on my way to Austin. Well, as I was bouncing around California getting additional training in ministry, I learned of a church plant happening in Austin, and I decided to help out.

That's how I ended up driving some dusty stretch of Texas highway with a parched, half-starved stranger in my car.

I whipped into the first gas station we passed for some drinks and snacks. I've never seen two Slim Jims and a forty-four-ounce Big Gulp Fanta Orange bring one person so much joy. Juan crashed the rest of the way, snoring up a storm from my passenger seat.

By the time we passed through San Antonio, it was nearly midnight. Juan had me drop him off behind the chain restaurant where he worked. "Are you sure you don't want me to bring you home?" I asked. "I don't mind."

Juan pointed to a makeshift lean-to between the dumpster and the back wall. Underneath the lean-to, there was a mattress on top of some wooden pallets. "That's okay, my friend," Juan said. "This is home."

I drove away slowly, looking back. A cold drink and some snacks were nice, but I was still leaving Juan to sleep on a pile of scrap wood behind a diner that night. And wherever his son might be, he still needed help too.

The Bible says that whatever we do for the poor and struggling, we do for the Lord. I wanted to give Jesus something more than Slim Jims and orange pop. I didn't want to leave him to sleep next to a dumpster.

Conviction ate me up later when I tried to pray. I wanted to help Juan get a roof over his head and a real bed and do whatever it took to find his son. I'm God's kid too. Look at how far He came to rescue me.

But that sort of help would take much more money and resources than I had. The way God kept putting people in my path, I felt sure I was called to do something more.

But how? I barely had enough to help myself.

.   .   .

Austin, Texas, is expensive, and I burned through my savings faster than planned. The good thing about restaurant experience is that you can always find work . . . except, I discovered, in Austin.

Eventually, I applied at the Italian steakhouse in the JW Marriott downtown. At least the manager agreed to bring me in for an interview. "So, Jimmy," he said, reading my name off the application. "Tell me a little bit about yourself."

Before I knew it, the stories were spilling out: blind eyes opened and crooked legs made straight. I told the manager how my back had been healed under the YWAM tent that night in Hawaii. I was talking way too much for a job interview at a fine-dining restaurant in one of the nicest hotels in Austin.

The manager just sat there, nodding along. I thought he was about to tell me they'd keep my application on file and let me know if a position came open. Instead, he shook my hand and offered me a job.

The Marriott's customers were very nice. One day, some guy left me a hundred-dollar tip, and it blew me apart. I didn't do anything to deserve it. He'd ordered the buffet. All I did was bring him orange juice. When I saw that Franklin on the table, I almost started tearing up. It's one thing to get a bonus from your boss—but that kind of blessing from a stranger? That's the feeling I wanted to share with the world.

I'd give my tips to a homeless woman who hung out near the JW Marriott sometimes, but I knew if I wanted to be able to change a person's life, it would take more money than I could earn working for someone else.

An entrepreneur named Ryan Moran had a series of YouTube videos on how to generate a passive income stream by selling products on Amazon. All I had to do was buy a product in bulk, package it, create a listing, and ship the stock to Amazon, which took a small cut of sales.

"But you have to find the *right* product," Ryan taught in his video. "That's the key."

· · ·

Fidget spinners were the red-hot fad of 2016, supposedly good for those struggling with ADHD. I ordered a few hundred wholesale and made a listing to sell online. Except the ones I got didn't spin right and cracked easily. I ended up having to offer so many refunds that Amazon nearly shut down my page. The returns went to my parents' house, and then all those boxes of broken fidget spinners ended up in my trunk.

I tried a few other products. No success. If I kept blowing stacks on failures, I would become the person needing financial help.

Since parking in downtown Austin costs about three hundred dollars a month, I had to walk to work from my apartment across the Colorado River, over in East Riverside. Except I worked the breakfast shift, so my "walk" was more like a mad sprint. I'd never had to get up that early before and became a habitual snooze button smasher. The Marriott's restaurant was fancy. Picture a lanky kid with a bad case of bed head booking it down East Second

Street in black dress pants and jacket, looking like I was either late for a wedding or running away from one.

A famous bumper sticker there says KEEP AUSTIN WEIRD. I was doing my part. As the weather turned colder, I ran to work, freezing and sweating at the same time. After my shift, I would walk back slower, thinking and talking to God.

One afternoon, I was trying to come up with the perfect product to sell on Amazon after a string of recent bombs. While walking across the bridge, I noticed some amateur artist had taken a Sharpie and drawn a mouse on the concrete barrier below.

Hmm, I thought. *That's interesting.*

When I got back to my apartment, I started looking up mousetraps. There was this new contraption from China with a tiny plank out over a bucket. You'd bait the plank with cheese, and when the mouse walked out on the end to get it, he (or she) would tip into the bucket. The cute and colorful trap was a more humane way of catching mice instead of killing them, like the old-fashioned sticky traps or spring-loaded bars that left you with a whacked rodent.

The next night, I was driving through downtown Austin. *Okay, God,* I prayed. *If You want me to do the mousetraps, send me a sign.* Does that sound crazy? Jesus said to pray about everything and talk to God like a good father. A good dad cares about every part of his kid's life. There's nothing off-limits or too small for the Lord.

At the next red light, a mouse ran across the street. Would you call that a sign? How about when a hundred more ran behind him a few seconds later? Because that's exactly what happened. I prayed for a sign about mouse-traps and a horde of mice dashed in front of my car.

After further research, I ordered something like five hundred traps at eighty cents apiece. Once they arrived, I hired a photographer to create packaging and content and named my first product "No Mice!" ("A safe, humane alternative that's four times more efficient than ordinary mousetraps!")

Although Amazon prohibits using family and friends to generate false reviews, it was obvious that everybody else was doing it, at least to get started. Uncles, great-aunts, distant cousins, old roommates—I reached out to anyone I could think of to ask for a five-star review.

It didn't work. The few I sold got terrible reviews saying the trap broke or didn't tip when the mouse got the cheese. There were a bunch of returns. No Mice! never got off the ground. I guess I ended up titling the product correctly, because I don't think any mice were caught.

I knew better than to fake reviews. When I was four-teen and trying to break into social media, I bought a thousand subscribers for a hundred bucks. Turned out they were all bots. Instead of moving me forward, that dirty little move set me back.

I should've learned my lesson then. I can't expect favor while taking shortcuts and compromising my integrity. God's not going to bless a cheat.

I thought I'd chosen the right thing and something that God was going to be proud of—a humane mousetrap. I figured that at some point, you have to do what the business world is doing in order to succeed. But would you drink a glass of water with a teaspoon of poison in it? Of course not. God is looking for things to be done with the utmost integrity and purity. If you want to launch things, then you've got to do things *His* way, not yours. It's like the Lord was looking down and shaking His head, saying, *Jimmy, you're on your own with this one.*

That One Moment When I Knew What I Was Called to Do

He who oppresses the poor reproaches his Maker,
but he who honors Him has mercy on the needy.

—PROVERBS 14:31

One afternoon on my walk home from the Marriott, I met a homeless senior citizen named Mr. Tony near my apartment. He wasn't asking for money or help, just sitting there on the corner with his head down, minding his own business. I love to sit cross-legged on the sidewalk and listen to people's stories, learning from their wisdom and asking questions about their lives.

Mr. Tony told me he couldn't even remember how long he'd been out on the streets. His clothes were ragged and his shoes had holes in the toes and the soles were coming loose. Austin is flat. When winter hits, the wind will whip down city streets and put a chill in your bones that's hard to shake.

"Hey, Mr. Tony, I was thinking about heading over to the Goodwill," I said. "You want to come along?"

After the No Mice! disaster, I didn't have much cash to spare, but you could always get someone fixed up at Goodwill: pants, shirts, and shoes. We picked out a pile of clothes, and I stood outside the dressing room while Mr. Tony tried them on. I could hear him struggling inside.

"You need some help?" I called.

No response.

I knocked and leaned closer to the door, listening. "Yeah," he admitted.

I cracked the door and slipped inside. Mr. Tony was standing there, awkward and silent, his shirt half undone. He was too old and brittle to change in and out of clothes without assistance.

Gently, I slid each shirtsleeve off his thin arms, careful not to cause him any pain. He leaned against my shoulder for support as I unfastened the buttons and helped him step out of his stained brown slacks.

The dressing room was hot, and his clothes smelled sour, like sweat and urine and grime. I said a silent prayer in that tiny Goodwill stall with the intercom calling for price checks and shoppers right outside the door and college kids laughing—but I can't tell you that angels sang or Jesus said, *Well done, My good and faithful servant.* I didn't get Spirit-filled goose bumps or a vision or a miracle word of knowledge.

But in that moment, I did feel sure of this: God called me to do what I was doing right then. To love the old, the poor, the fragile and frail. Walking in love means you show up to help, whatever that may be. You do what needs to be done and make sure that person feels as human and loved and appreciated as possible.

We've all made a mess of ourselves. God knocks at the door. We lean on Jesus while we step out of our mess. We hold on while He helps us change because we're not capable of changing ourselves.

There were no engagement likes, algorithms, subscribers, or shares. No one was watching. Nobody knew but Mr. Tony and God—and that's exactly how it should've been. It's funny how we can make ourselves feel good about doing things we're supposed to do. Serving others should be an everyday part of life, as natural as brushing our teeth.

Once I helped Mr. Tony get dressed in new clothes and shoes, his whole expression changed. Smiling, brighter. Like a new man.

"Hey, you hungry?" I asked.

"Sure am, yeah."

"Where you want to go?"

"Anywhere's good," he replied. "You pick."

Your Idol Is Finally Dead

The steps of a good man are ordered by the LORD, and He
delights in his way. Though he fall, he shall not be utterly
cast down; for the LORD upholds him with His hand.

—PSALM 37:23–24

After seven months in Austin, I headed back to California
to do more ministry schooling, splitting the rent with a
fellow ministry student named Ray. The best we could
afford was a little apartment over on Placer Street, in the
rougher part of Redding. There were parties and police
sirens all the time. Our roommate's bike was immediately
stolen. Homeless people would pound on our door, and
everything smelled like weed. Even though Ray and I
didn't partake, the neighbors would smoke out front and
fumes would pour in through our vents. One time, a six-
foot-three guy who looked like a WWE wrestler took
my parking spot. We left a note under his windshield
wiper to "confront" him and locked our door. Probably
not the brightest idea, but we lived to write this book.

I was still completely off social media, but Ray started filming videos of life around our apartment complex. Ray had about six hundred followers, but they all seemed to absolutely love it.

Ray likes to clown as much as I do, so we were a good match, stirring each other up to do something wild. We'd have rap battles at one A.M., with Christmas lights flashing and a fog machine going until the smoke alarm triggered and our neighbors banged on the wall and yelled for us to go to bed. Ray would throw our furniture into the dumpster, and I'd run outside and shout something like, "Oh, no! That was Grandma Clarissa's favorite chair! She told us never to throw it away!"

We might have been ministry students, but we were also college kids out on our own. I still loved a good prank and the rush of adrenaline, as long as the joke was on ourselves.

One afternoon during school, a local leader, Hannah, approached me saying she had a prophetic word to share. We walked to the back of the sanctuary to avoid disturbing my classmates.

Before Hannah started, I grabbed my phone, brought up Voice Memos, and hit the red button to record the prophecy she had for me. "Hello, future Jimmy," I whispered.

"December fourth, 2018," Hannah began. "At 3:13 P.M.

So saith the Lord . . . you will have a TV show. And the Lord is creating a support system for you. Yes. Family and friends who will cover you. Discernment and protection. People to lean on."

She paused, listening.

"I also see you walking through only the doors the Lord has opened and to the people He has called you to. You're not the mouse in the room. You're the elephant . . . and that's good because elephants are very loyal and funny and kind. And they stand out. Jimmy, you are loved."

"Amen," I replied softly. "Thank you so much."

I played Hannah's word repeatedly, breaking it down. Prophecies didn't always hit the bull's-eye, especially at school. Could "TV show" mean YouTube or some other platform? Didn't matter—I'd quit making videos anyway. But if God wanted to put me on TV, what kind of show would that be?

I remembered a conversation I'd had a year prior with my friend Ryan. I told him I wanted to give away a million dollars and houses and cars and travel around on a mission to make people's day. That's the kind of show I wanted to make.

With one zing, Ryan brought me back down to earth. "Jimmy," he said, "you gotta be Santa Claus in private before you can ever be Santa in public."

I knew what Ryan was saying, but why not take the

extra step and go full-on Santa? I already had a Santa Claus suit, but the only beard I could find was scraggly and brown. Imagine a tall, skinny Santa with a dirty brown beard cruising the streets of California at night, hanging with the homeless, breakdancing with strangers in the produce section of Walmart. Showing up in that famous red-and-white suit changes the atmosphere. Everybody loves Santa. God's prankster, Saint Nick, on the prowl at grocery stores and 7-Elevens, looking for someone to bless.

·   ·   ·

Once I settled back in California, I chose a simple little inexpensive product to sell on Amazon, something from an industry I was familiar with—restaurant equipment. This time, I promised that I would not cheat or take shortcuts. I still wasn't sure how a new Amazon product would succeed without some boost. Better to fail following God than win by being dishonest, though, right?

One day, I was spending time with the Lord when I heard His voice.

Give ten thousand dollars away.

What? I thought. *No way*—$10k was nearly half of my savings, something I'd been building up for twenty years.

I kept ignoring the message, thinking it was probably just my own mind stirring up some legalistic thought. Days passed and I still felt the pull to give. I couldn't talk to my parents or anyone else about it, because it would sound ridiculous.

Shoot, if I've gone this far in life trusting God's voice, then I might as well continue, I finally thought. I need to give Jesus authority over everything in my life. I had already given up videos and other things. Managing and saving money is good, but when God tells me to give something away, the only right response is to give.

Around this time, Pastor Rick (from back in Minnesota) and his wife, Robin, were planning a mission trip around the country. Mission trips take money, and I knew they would steward it well. I put the money in an envelope and slipped it to Pastor Rick.

I'm not saying this to brag. Or if so, I'm bragging on God, because two weeks later my Amazon sales began to climb, this time with verified five-star reviews. That passive income stream allowed me to start helping others even more, wherever I saw a need.

That's when the revelation hit me. If your fist is squeezed tight around your money, you're preventing yourself from using it to help others. You can't receive God's blessing with a closed fist, but if our hands stay open to give, they are also open to receive.

"Jimmy, you know that envelope you gave me?" Pastor Rick told me years later. "It's still full."

"What the heck, you didn't spend even a dollar?"

"Oh, we did. If we saw a young mom buying groceries, we'd give her two hundred bucks. If we met someone who needed gas, we would fill their tank. But then we'd meet someone else, and they would give us five hundred dollars. So, the envelope never ran dry."

"*Daaang.* That's candy." What else could I say?

.   .   .

Our apartment was close to a range of foothills with a trail winding up to a view of Mount Shasta. One afternoon, I was up on the hilltop talking to Jesus, trying to figure out what to do with my life. Ministry? Comedy? Sales? Missionary work?

The pressure from my family to land on a career was getting intense. I had always dreamed of finding a way to travel the world while combining entertainment with evangelism, but in that moment, all the desire seemed gone. I was totally content being a pizza driver.

I kept talking to God, thanking Him for the mountains and trees and clear blue skies, rolling hills all the way to the Pacific Ocean, wildflowers covering the valley like a carpet of purple and gold.

A grandma and her six-year-old grandson were out walking and came up from an area I'd never seen people come from before. I asked the boy, "What are you thankful for?"

I thought he'd say something like "a toy," but instead he told me, "Everything!" I'd never heard anyone say that in my life. It gave me such a simple perspective.

God and Adam used to walk in the garden like friends. That's what it felt like that afternoon: as if the Lord was right there alongside me, and the rest of the world and its problems faded away. It didn't matter if I washed dishes for the rest of my life. I'd rather be rolling silverware with the Lord in small-town Minnesota than rolling down Sunset Boulevard in a McLaren, thriving in the world's eyes but miles away from contentment. There is no joy like God's peace. Friendship with Jesus is all I will ever need.

"I don't care if I ever make another video again," I told the Lord. "I'm totally fine living in the middle of nowhere, with no one ever knowing who I am, just living a quiet life with You."

Out of the stillness, God spoke to my heart.

Okay, Jimmy, He said. *Your idol is finally dead.*

"What do you mean?" I asked. "I thought I killed my idol years ago when I deleted all my videos?"

That's when the Lord said to me, *No, externally that is what you did. But now, internally your idol is dead.*

That is what the Lord is after. Our hearts.

IV

Lil' Bit of Kindness

This Is How You Start

You don't have to be great to start,
but you have to start to be great.

—ZIG ZIGLAR

God had one more word after telling me that my idol was finally dead.

Now go make videos for Me.

I thought I had let go of that dream years before, but until that moment on the hill, it was still a seed in my heart. When I fully surrendered, God gave it back, and I couldn't wait to start creating content again.

By then, Ray was not only my best friend. He had also become engaged to my sister Chelsie, after she had moved to California.

"Hey, God wants me to make videos again," I told Ray. "Can we do one together?"

"Ya, bro," said Ray, "for sure."

"All right, here's what it's going to be. We're going to

play each other in basketball. Loser has to get blindfolded and tattooed with whatever the winner wants."

Ray just nodded, totally unfazed. "Sounds good."

I was laughing inside as we bumped fists to seal the deal. Ray's a skateboarding surfer dude. He couldn't ball to save his life.

Ray represented the Utah Jazz while I wore my Sixers jersey. First one to eleven points gets the W. My future brother-in-law took an early lead, six to one. By halftime, I'd closed the gap. We brought a stranger out and promised to give him a hundred bucks if he could make a free throw, but his shoulder was messed up, so we laid hands on him and prayed before continuing the game. This is what I finally felt what the Lord meant when He said to make videos for Him.

I was just holding back earlier to mess with Ray's mind. After halftime, he never made another shot. Final score, eleven to six.

We rolled up to Xtreme Cycles and Tattooz. Ray and Chelsie were holding hands, all cute and happy, like young Christians who knew they were about to get married soon. I blindfolded them both before we walked in.

The tattoo artist was a big guy. Just out of prison. I pulled him to the side so I could tell him about my idea for Ray's tattoo. "You sure?" he asked, cutting his eyes toward the happy couple and shaking his head.

"Do it!"

Tattoo Guy grabbed his ink gun and went to work on Ray's upper thigh. I was straight up cackling while rapid-fire needles stung Ray's skin and he grimaced and vise-gripped Chelsie's hand. Forty minutes of tense hilarity passed.

"Okay, blindfolds off. Time for the reveal."

From just above Ray's kneecap, nearly to his hip, was a tattooed picture of me pointing and scowling at him. Right below were the words DON'T TOUCH HER!!! I put my name on there too, of course. It was as big as this book!

Chelsie flipped out so bad I thought she was going to punch me in the throat. "Now I have to look at my brother's face every night!" she said.

They should be thankful. I almost got my entire family permanently inked on Ray.

I edited our one-on-one tattoo challenge video for maximum laughs, emphasizing the part where we shared the Gospel. It was the first new Jimmy Darts video uploaded to social media in four years. Even though we stopped in the middle of our game to pray, the comments were all like, *LOL, that was sooo wrong.*

I had a couple more ideas to try. I ran through Manhattan dressed like Buddy the Elf and got thrown out of the Empire State Building, trying to illustrate the importance of being childlike, which the Bible calls us to be. Sticking with the holiday theme, I found a white beard to go with my Santa suit and filmed a video giving away weird Christmas gifts to college kids—stuff like an electric steam cooker and a broken dog clock. I kept having to pull my Santa pants back up, but the clips were clean, and I reminded people that God's greatest gift ever is Jesus because He loves us and wants to be our friend.

The reaction was mostly laughing emojis and *LOL,* although several commenters asked *How can this not be viral,* and I had the same question. Nothing I uploaded got more than a few thousand views. I realized my videos weren't making the impact I had hoped when the comments reflected they weren't doing anything other than giving people a good laugh.

I think most of us struggle with how to aim high while staying realistic. It's the balance between chasing dreams and reaching for God's best. The Lord gives all of us unique talents and desires. Just be the person He made you to be, right?

Sometimes figuring that out is the toughest part.

.   .   .

After my second year in ministry school, I moved back home with my parents again. They probably thought, *The prodigal son keeps coming back. Pretty soon, he's going to be thirty and still living upstairs, making fart videos and dressing like an elf.*

"Jimmy," my dad said. "What do you want to do with your life?" I was back waiting tables in his restaurant and from the tone of his voice, it was clear he didn't think I was called to the family business.

"If I could do anything?" I asked. "*Anything?*"

My dad nodded.

"I want to go around the country and give away more money than anyone has ever given away before. And I want to make videos about it that are fun and that point people to God."

My dad is old-school, practical, the kind of man who works hard all day, every day, and doesn't complain. I wasn't sure what he'd think of my dream. "All right, Jimmy." He clapped his hands and looked me in the eye. "Then get started."

Get started? I'd already been halfway around the world on mission trips and here I was back hustling for tips at Jimmy's Restaurant. Get started where? When? How?

"If that's what you want to do, don't waste time chasing plan B or C," my dad told me. "Start working on your dream now. Just go. *Go!*"

The next day, I was walking the block with Ray, unloading all this on him, and trying to decide what to do differently if I didn't want to end up waiting tables at my family's restaurant when I was forty-five. As soon as we stepped foot in my driveway, Facebook dinged. Some random viewer sent this long message about how a video I'd put out had helped her laugh again and see the good in people. I was like, *What the heck? Despite my silly pranks, something touched a stranger's life thousands of miles away?*

That's when the lightning struck. The Lord spoke—not out loud, but deep inside, where it counts. *Wake up, Jimmy. This is how you start.*

The following morning, I hit up my pal Johnny Buckets to come along and help film. Buckets was home-schooled and never got out of the house much, so he was down to see something other than the view from his back porch.

We jumped into the car and started driving cross-country on a mission to take over TikTok for God's glory, and it shot to the top of social media platforms during the pandemic. I'd been watching these viral comedy videos made by two friends who called themselves the Cheeky Boyos. They would take challenges from the internet, like *Go to Olive Garden and don't say no to the parmesan until it's a mountain.* In another funny clip, fans dared them to join a biker gang.

From my past videos of pranks and clowning around, I knew I could do a family-friendly version of this. I knew if I could get some momentum and an audience, I could gain the resources to give back like I truly wanted. I began by asking viewers to submit challenges in my comments section. Since I was starting fresh with no viewers, I created a random account so I could send myself challenges, like *Go up to a stranger and give them something without saying a word.*

I had some packing tape on the back seat floorboard. I saw a woman parked at the grocery store with the windows down, so I walked over and handed her the roll of tape without saying anything.

"Are you serious?" she said. "We were trying to find some tape to mail my package!" She was freaking out. "We just left the post office and they didn't have any!"

Just then, her husband walked out of the store. "Jerry!" she shouted. "This kid just gave me some tape!"

He looked the situation over, eyebrows raised. "Where'd you come from?" Jerry asked.

"He's an *angel!*" his wife replied.

I was freaking out too, but the challenge said I had to stay silent. I nodded, smiled, and got back in my car thinking, *No way that's just a coincidence. God is all over this.*

Because of her reaction, thousands upon thousands of views poured in. Right out of the gate, we were cooking. After that, the challenges started to roll in on their own.

I was on the way to Mount Rushmore when *Propose to a stranger* showed up in my comments. With a crowd milling around the observation deck a few hundred feet beneath Abe Lincoln's chin, I raised my hand.

"Excuse me, everybody!" I said. "I would like to draw your attention away from Mount Rushmore for a second. I've found something that's much more beautiful than that."

Everybody stopped to see what I was talking about. I turned to a woman in her late fifties with curly gray hair and a flower-print blouse. "I think I've met the girl of my dreams!" I proclaimed, before dropping to one knee and holding out a sparkly ring from the thrift store.

Gazing deeply into her eyes, I popped the question. "Will you marry me?"

"I'm already married," she replied. "He's right over there."

I stood quickly. A brawny, bald-headed man bounded up to me. "What's going on here?" he demanded.

"Oh, sorry," I said softly, shrinking from six one to about five foot eight. "I was looking at the wrong hand."

A hush fell over the crowd. Even George Washington was looking down his nose and waiting to see my fate.

The bald man's scowl melted into a smile. "I'll pay for your honeymoon," he said with a laugh.

"Ohh, baby!" I replied, relieved that I wasn't gonna get my neck wrung.

His wife cracked up and then their teenage daughter walked over and started laughing at me too. "I could've been your dad!" I told her.

Was it stupid? Sure. Funny? People must have thought so because my videos started racking up views, building with each post. Meanwhile, the challenges kept coming.

Go to Domino's and ask to use their phone to call Pizza Hut and get a pizza delivered.

Go to Walmart and let a kid pick out any toy they want.

Sit with a random family eating at Denny's and say, "Sorry I'm late."

Find someone walking their dog and say, "Sprinkles, oh my goodness, I've been looking everywhere for you!"

Did you know that Pizza Hut will actually deliver to Domino's? That was fun. It was all fun. Expensive too. Telling a kid she can get any toy she wants makes a great video, but it costs about a hundred and fifty bucks.

We lived as cheap as possible, eating PB&J and scrubbing the road dust off with slivers of borrowed soap in some lake or river at the end of the day. Sometimes we would sleep in a little tent pitched on the side of the road. Other times we'd recline the seats back and catch a few hours in some Walmart parking lot.

Eventually, we had to head back home to Minnesota. Between travel costs and giving away money, I couldn't afford to stay on the road. I had momentum though. And a whole lot of viewers waiting to see what I would do next.

Okay, I prayed. *How can I use this to change somebody's life?*

No Security

Be strong and of good courage; do not be afraid,
nor be dismayed, for the LORD your God is
with you wherever you go.

—JOSHUA 1:9

After I returned, a friend from ministry school, Big
Johnny (Maura, not Buckets) contacted me about a home
security system business that he'd just joined in Jacksonville, Florida.

"Come on down," Big Johnny said. "You know how
to talk to people, Jimmy. You'd be a natural in sales. Besides, it'll be a lot of fun."

I was torn but said yes. I wanted to get married someday soon and have a family. You can't sleep in the car and
live on peanut butter while raising children. I don't think
my future wife would be okay with that. And I did like
talking to people. Big Johnny said I could climb the cor-
porate ladder and make a good living in high-commission
sales.

On one hand, my videos were steadily building to a million-plus views every time I put out a new clip. Going up to strangers in Denny's and apologizing to them for being late as I sat next to them got over *ten million views.* On the other hand, I was twenty-four. That's late for an influencer to be starting. How much longer could I chase my childhood dream? An opportunity was waiting. A job with security. (Literally.)

The next day, I got a call from a company called the Adventure Challenge. They put out books filled with spontaneous challenges to help couples have fun and get to know each other better. The Adventure Challenge was based in Redding, California. The owner was an alumni of the same ministry school I had graduated from.

"Jimmy, we love your videos where people send challenges to you in the comments," their rep said. "We want to hire you to do a video where you take a girl on a crazy date and promote our scratch-off book of fun challenges."

A date? I thought. *I've never even had a girlfriend. I'm not afraid to talk to strangers, though, so . . .*

"Yeah, I'm down for that," I replied.

Adventure Challenge agreed to pay me a thousand bucks to make the video. They'd send out a copy of the book for me, but I had to pay for the date myself. There were no guidelines, and the challenges weren't extravagant. It could be a ten-dollar date. That was up to me.

I was just happy to be getting paid to make a video. When someone is willing to give you money to do what you love, it gives your dream value. It's confirmation that you can rise out of amateur status someday.

The problem was that confirmation of my dream job arrived just as I was about to leave to start a normal, steady job. If Adventure Challenge had called a day earlier, I probably would've taken it as a sign to head for California. But a call coming in right before I'm leaving for another job in Florida?

Hmm, the company was called Adventure Challenge—what if that's a clue? What if it's all in God's time and this is simply part of my challenge and adventure? Why did I have to let go of either one? If you're young and grinding, you don't have to let any opportunity slip away. At this point, I realized not to over-spiritualize things, but to do what I knew God had already called me to do.

The next morning, I headed south, flying down I-75, windows open, talking to God, trying to figure out what I should do. I shot content for my channel on the road trip. Each video blew up, going viral, keeping me torn.

Once I arrived in Jacksonville, Big Johnny handed me a bright orange polo shirt with a lanyard badge identifying me as JAMES KELLOGG—SALES.

Sales, as in walking around a neighborhood knocking on doors and trying to get whoever answered to buy a high-priced home security system. Most people would rather wrestle rattlesnakes than knock on a stranger's door, but it didn't bother me. A few months earlier, I'd made a video asking random Walmart shoppers if I could wax their chests. (Just guys. Not trying to go to jail.) Trying to sell security systems seemed easy compared to that.

Plus, I love meeting new people. That turned out to be the problem. I'd talk to potential customers for an hour, even if it was clear they weren't going to buy anything.

Man, I thought. *I gotta find a way to cut to the chase and get some clear yeses and noes.*

One morning, I met Jeff. Super-nice guy. Jeff was interested in a security system to protect his wife and kids. We talked for a long time about family and God and life in northern Florida compared to northern Minnesota. (One's too cold and the other's too hot.)

Jeff explained that as much as he'd sleep better at night knowing his wife and children had that extra level of security, the system was something he simply could not afford. *Uh-oh, that's a pretty clear no.*

Still, it was nice of Jeff to stand there talking to some green kid from Minnesota going door-to-door trying to sell alarms. Most people wouldn't even answer the door, much less go out of their way to make a salesman feel better about himself. I wanted to do something nice for Jeff too.

I went on Instagram Live and told my viewers what a good guy Jeff was and how he wanted to protect his family. Then I put up Jeff's Venmo and asked people to help if they felt led. I was so excited when viewers pledged a grand total of two hundred dollars to help. And you know what? Jeff *still* didn't buy a security system.

This was not great. There I was, walking up and down neighborhood streets in the hot Florida sun, shirt drenched with sweat—and nobody was buying what I had to sell.

I knew I could get better at sales if I really worked at it, but then I had a conversation with my dad. "You can get a sales job at the snap of a finger anytime in your life," he told me. "That's not a rare opportunity. But your videos have momentum right now. You've got to go all in on your dream and give it a chance." As Leonard Ravenhill says, "The opportunity of a lifetime must be seized during the lifetime of the opportunity."

.   .   .

My dad's words were still in my head when it came time to make that dating video for the company in California. One shot to prove my value, and I knew it had to be a home run. I decided not to preplan anything. I'd find an absolute stranger and take her on the craziest date ever.

I went to the mall and walked right up to someone that looked just like my grandma but didn't need a cane, dressed in a Juicy tracksuit. She laughed in my face and said no. But I knew that no would look good on video.

Next, I found two girls who appeared closer to my age. "Hey, how's it goin'?" I said. We talked a bit. "I was wondering if you'd maybe want to go on a date with me?"

They started giggling and looking at each other like I'd lost my mind. They knew that it was all in good fun because I showed them the book and explained how I needed a stranger to complete the challenge. The taller girl had long brown hair, a floral-print face mask, and big expressive eyes that sparked with curiosity. "A date, huh?" she said. "Sure, okay. Whatever."

We met up the following afternoon. First, we went to Goodwill and picked out each other's outfits for the day. I put her in a bright purple trench coat. Since I was from Minnesota, she made me wear an extra-small Green Bay Packers jersey. The bottom hit about a foot above my belly button.

We went to the park and spent some time seeing who could go higher on the swings. I had an indoor skydiving session booked for later, but the video still didn't have enough big, crazy moments to hold viewers' attention. It's a good thing I had a trunk filled with enough fireworks for a small town's Fourth of July.

At the end of the night, I edited two and a half hours of video down to the best minute and uploaded it to my feeds. While waiting, I added up my expenses.

Dang it, this date cost more than I made!

The next morning, I was back walking the streets of some sleepy neighborhood looking for sales. I checked to see how the video was doing. One million views.

I knocked on a few doors, talking to strangers, trying to work in the sales pitch. Between houses, I checked again. Two million views.

Then three million.

It kept on building. And building . . . At the end of the day, the representative from Adventure Challenge called.

"Eleven million views, Jimmy! I *knew* taking a chance on you was the right thing to do!" I could picture him, fists pumping, pacing back and forth in front of his desk while we talked. "I had a feeling God was going to do a *miracle* with this video. We just had one of the top sales days in our company's existence. We don't see these numbers except on Black Friday. Hallelujah!"

Or at least I think he said "hallelujah"? Bottom line, the video was a huge success. I got a ton of new followers and didn't have to compromise my message. There was no kissing or anything creepy or suggestive. I don't think viewers like that kind of stuff anyway. Deep down, we all want something uplifting, emotional, and real.

"Now, Jimmy, listen," the rep continued. "Adventure Challenge is all in. We want to hire you to do five more videos. This time, it's five thousand dollars a pop. All expenses paid."

The next day, I told Big Johnny that the security business wasn't for me. He just laughed. I never got one sale.

"You got the bagel, Jimmy," Big Johnny said, making a zero with his hands. "Big zero, nothing. You didn't even get any cream cheese on it."

· · ·

Sales career = no dollars. Making videos = also no dollars . . . yet. But a paying job was waiting and that was confirmation enough for me.

For my next big dating challenge, I took a girl to Dubai, knowing I'd have to raise the stakes and make the video even crazier. We rented a Lamborghini to see the city's jaw-dropping ultramodern architecture and ended up on a skydiving expedition over that giant palm-tree-shaped island. From eating peanut butter out of the jar and sleeping in my Honda to driving a Lambo through the most glamorous city in the world. Wild times.

Coulda passed on the skydiving, though. I'm scared of heights and wasn't paying attention when the instructor told us what to do after jumping out of the plane. I just figured on praying really hard. Anyway, I didn't lift my head, so the wind hit me in the face at 120 mph and I couldn't breathe. Then my instructor pulled the ripcord and it got tangled.

I was tripping out over skyscrapers and feeling like I might be meeting Jesus a lot sooner than I thought. *Oh, crap,* I thought. *I'm never even gonna get to have kids.*

Best Friends for the Day

There is a friend who sticks closer than a brother.

—PROVERBS 18:24

I popped down from Jacksonville to Miami to see my parents, who were on vacation, when a challenge came in.

Become best friends with a stranger for the day!?????
CRAZYPABZ

The challenge had thousands of likes, so the next day at breakfast, I told my dad, "I'm going to look for a friend." I didn't have a plan other than to be open to God and have fun. God is fun. When everybody's laughing, hearts are open. Fun turns us all into kids again.

I was walking down the beach when I saw this guy sitting by a little blue tent, wearing a do-rag, no shirt, and the same Adidas slides as me. He was staring at the water, the only other person alone on the beach.

"Hey, bro," I said. "You wanna hang out and be best friends for the day? My name's Jimmy."

"I'm Yah," he replied suspiciously, returning my fist bump.

"I hardly have any friends," I added. "I just moved to Florida."

His suspicion vanished, replaced by a friendly smile. "Sure, why not? We could do something."

Yah hopped into my car and we drove off with the windows down. I told him up front that I was filming for TikTok. "That's cool," he said. We saw a couple of kids shooting hoops in a nearby park, so we joined them for some half-court two-on-two.

"Hey, you hungry?" I asked Yah after a few games.

"Yeah," he replied. "Come on, I know a place where we can get some food."

We jumped a fence into an empty field. Apparently if you're hungry enough, there's a certain kind of grass you can eat to survive. I don't know if that's what Yah was doing, but he showed me how to find a little clover-looking plant. I broke a piece off and started chewing. "Tastes like Sour Patch Kids," I told him.

Yah laughed. "Jimmy, man, you're trippin' me out."

After a bit of wild greens, we went for pasta at an Italian place down the street. Yah mentioned that he liked to skate, so we hit up the roller rink next, just chilling, laughing, talking about God and life. Even though he'd been through some major disappointments and difficult times, he was still a fun-loving, easygoing guy.

At the end of the day, I was driving Yah back to his tent. Traffic slowed my Honda to a crawl. I glanced over, and he was looking out the side window, choking back tears. "Jimmy," Yah said, "when you met me on the beach, I was at a place in life where I felt empty. It felt like I was dying, man."

I didn't say anything back, giving him space.

"That's why I came to the beach to live. I was just gonna put my faith in God and believe He could find a way for me. Then you showed up. Today changed my whole perspective on life."

I kept driving, thinking, nodding to let Yah know I was listening. I hadn't given him any money. I was just being his friend. He was a nice guy who'd made some mistakes and was trying to find his way. I knew what that was like. "Hey, you got Cash App?" I asked.

"I do," he replied.

"I'm gonna put your Cash App at the end of this video so my followers can see it," I said. "Let's see what happens."

When I got home, I edited the video, cutting the footage down to tell the best story, showing how much fun we'd had, but being careful not to hurt Yah's dignity or make myself look like the hero. I was the kid with no friends. Yah had been helping me.

I uploaded our clip before dinner with my parents. By bedtime, the video only had ten thousand views. *Man, that's terrible,* I thought. *TikTok is probably mad that I'm trying to raise money. I should probably delete it in the morning.*

When I woke up, I checked the video again. Nine million views and climbing. *What?*

He ended up with around $20K! I double-checked to make sure I was seeing right before shooting Yah a text. *Bro, check your Cash App. I think you might have a little Christmas present in there.*

This is crazy! he messaged back. *They sent so much!!!* I was stunned that so many people had reached out, that God had let me be part of something so cool.

Later that day, Yah and I met up at a McDonald's near the beach. He showed me how his phone had been blowing up with one comment after another wishing him the best. "They love you," I told him. "Anything you want to say?"

Yah looked into my phone camera, trying to speak but overwhelmed. "You've blessed me with the opportunity of a lifetime," he finally told the viewers, "and I just want to thank all of you for helping me. I pray God will bless you in return."

Yah used the money to travel and pass the blessing on. Beyond that, I'm not sure. Bless people and leave the rest to God—no strings attached. I wouldn't be surprised if somewhere along the way, Yah reached out to be someone's best friend for the day.

That video didn't just change his life, it changed the way I thought about making videos. On a whim, I had invited the viewers in on my dream of helping folks who needed it. The focus was on others, not me. Just the way I wanted it and exactly the way it needed to be.

It blew my mind that people would be so generous, and I started thinking—what if God just wants me to be a bridge, connecting people to people, sharing stories, sharing the fun, inviting everybody in? Isn't that what God is all about anyway? Inviting everybody in?

Being best friends with Yah for the day showed me that there are a lot of good-hearted people out there who want to give and be part of a better story. All I had to do was show a need.

And I think God was showing me how.

·   ·   ·

Some people see stories like this and comment how awesome it is that I'm on a mission to bless others. I feel like I'm the one who gets blessed. The joy I receive is a hundredfold, a thousandfold even.

There is always a lesson. The challenge was "be someone's best friend for the day"—maybe people wanted to see me acting silly or having fun in an awkward situation. Through that challenge, I was reminded that Jesus finds us where we are and asks to be our friend. Maybe He finds us lost or desperate or sad. He finds all of us needing a good friend, a listening ear, the kind of friendship that many of us have given up on looking for.

That's all I really want to do, introduce people to my good friend Jesus. The best way I've found to do that is simply to share what I've got, whether that's a laugh, some food, money. Pay attention. Listen instead of talk. It's simple, really. Small things.

Maybe you're reading this and coming from a different place, different background, different points of view. You might read your Bible and pray every day, or you might not even know what to think about God anymore. Either way, we can agree on one thing: we help one another down here, and when we do that, we are very close to the heart of God.

I believe God wants us to spend every day in fellowship, walking through this life with simple joy and trust in the only one who can guide us through. Each morning, the Lord holds out His hand.

"Want to hang out and be best friends for the day?"

V

Ohh, Baby

The Kindness Challenge

And let us not grow weary while doing good, for in
due season we shall reap if we do not lose heart.

—GALATIANS 6:9

After the success of the Adventure Challenge videos, I
decided to leave the security job behind and go all in. So,
I packed and moved to the land of big media dreams,
Southern California.

I was still thinking about the best friend challenge.
One small twist had sent that video over the top. It wasn't
just some random handout. Yah helped me first.

Then God dropped some wisdom on my heart.

*Jimmy, content about kindness and helping people has been
around forever. But it's usually centered around the person doing
it. Ask people for help. And if they help you, change their life.*
I started praying about a new approach. Rather than
going up to people and handing them money—I'd ask for
cash instead. Or food or gas. That's where my long history of stunts and pranks could come in handy. I've never

felt awkward approaching strangers. I love having to think on my feet and see where a strange situation takes me.

Videos where I gave out cash felt kinda cringe anyway. The Bible is clear that you should give without drawing attention to yourself. "But when you do a charitable deed, do not let your left hand know what your right hand is doing," Jesus said, "that your charitable deed may be in secret; and your Father who sees in secret will Himself reward you openly" (Matthew 6:3–4).

Too often, social media is all about me, me, me. Check out my clothes and my flex. But I could feel God telling me to spotlight others instead. There are wonderful, generous people everywhere you go, a common thread of kindness in the world that's rarely reflected in social media. Maybe I could do something about that.

All these thoughts were running through my head while I was walking down the sidewalk in Costa Mesa, talking to God. That's what I felt like He was telling me. A kindness test. Ask people for help, and when they respond, do your best to change their lives.

Just then, I saw a family crossing the street at the next intersection. There were five of them, two parents and three little kids, and they were speaking Spanish. *Why not start now?* I thought.

I cut left at the walk so we'd cross paths and flicked my

hidden camera on. "Excuse me," I said. "I hate to bother you, but I haven't eaten anything today and I'm just really hungry . . . if you have anything?"

The mom reached into her backpack and handed me a burrito. The dad gave me a dollar. They didn't even hesitate.

"Ohh, thank you so much," I said. "Here, now I've got something for you." I held out a hundred-dollar bill. The surprise on their faces was priceless, looking at one another, looking back at me.

"That's for helping me today," I explained. "You're amazing!"

Then we all stood there smiling and laughing and nodding at one another, and it wasn't even awkward. It's like it didn't matter that we couldn't speak each other's language.

When I edited the video, I knew that I had captured something special because I could still feel the joy of that moment, even when I was watching it on my phone. The surprise, their reactions. It was almost like I was playing a wholesome prank.

Through the comment section, I learned that the dad worked at a local restaurant. His community heard about the clip and started posting about how great it was to see him get recognized because they already knew he was a

kindhearted guy. Everybody started liking those comments, so they rose to the top, blessing the family even
more with words of encouragement.

After seeing the reactions, I realized that a hundred
bucks for a family of five wasn't much. So, I tracked down
the family and we paid their rent for a month. (I say "we"
because even back then, I had people who believed in
what I was doing and wanted to get in on the blessing.)

From there, it was easy and fun to come up with new
ideas. Find the first stranger willing to sing "Happy Birthday" to me. Cry in front of TJ Maxx and give a hundred
dollars to the first person who asks if I'm okay. Pretend
my car ran out of gas and see who'll help me push it to
the corner station.

Sure, I got turned down. A lot. Unless I got permission, I would cut that part out. I'm not about exposing
anyone. You never know what somebody's going through
or the reasons they might say no. After all, it's pretty weird
and unexpected to have someone approach you asking
for stuff.

But those moments when it worked were worth every
bit of rejection. Rewarding strangers for generosity is a
blast! Everything shifted once I started filming the kindness challenge. God was showing me a way to be both
careful and carefree, to have fun and be spontaneous

while helping others and changing lives. I finally felt like I was doing what I was born to do.

My social media channels blew up. I went from giving away a hundred dollars to five hundred to thousands through GoFundMes. From a million views to a million-plus followers, from regional to nationwide to around the world.

But it still felt like something was missing.

Something big.

Purity, Not Perfection

Do not stir up nor awaken love until it pleases.

—SONG OF SOLOMON 8:4

Since the day I got saved, I had not kissed a girl.

Yeah, I know that sounds kind of crazy. Check this out.

Several years ago, I watched a YouTube sermon on purity and the importance of guarding your heart. The speaker said that sex outside of God's plan can shipwreck your priorities. If a person truly wants to grab hold of their purpose, they will have to not only crucify the flesh but discipline the mind as well.

"When you see who He created you to be, you'll stop selling cheap what was paid for with a high price," Pastor Dan Mohler said. "Purity isn't about rules; it's about protecting what God values most—your heart."

As a single young man, I didn't need a sermon to remind me of the difficulties of lust. It's like being dipped in honey and told to cage-fight a bear. Many careers and ministries fall due to uncontrolled desires, and I knew that purity would be particularly key to my calling, so I played that YouTube sermon over and over again. After about a hundred repeats, the words worked their way past my ears and into my heart.

It felt like God was using that message to show me purity from a different perspective. The focus isn't white-knuckling your way through temptations and denying your desires. Living pure is less about what you miss out on and more about everything you gain from self-control.

A quality relationship cannot be built on the pursuit of sexual gratification. You're ignoring who a person is to obsess over what you want to do to them. How can that possibly work out for the good?

Once physical affection is off the table, you can concentrate on more important things. Do you really enjoy spending time with this person, talking, listening, and sharing the important parts of life? Are you spiritually and financially compatible? Could you take a long road trip together without driving each other crazy? Can you have fun and be your real, true self, whether you're VIP at Disney or sneaking onto the swings at the school playground? Sex can wreck not only your priorities but your judgment too. I could walk into an In-N-Out tomorrow and kiss ten people and feel an attraction to six of them.

That's not because I love them, but because of chemicals and our wiring.

No unmarried person wants to hear a sermon on purity. The way it's been talked about in church, I understand why. You get some couple telling you to save sex until the wedding night after they've been married for twenty-five years. The Bible doesn't say "manage the flesh," it says put the deeds of the flesh to death. That's why another verse says "It is good for a man not to touch a woman," and it doesn't mean "don't give her a high five." It means don't touch her with desire, and it's not good to go an inch because it means that you'll go a mile, when you're not married.

Often their marriage is a mess behind the scenes and the whole church knows it, but everybody sits there and pretends. And this is supposed to convince the youth group that they should wait?

Every goal requires self-control. If you're on a mission to get in shape, you can't throw it away with late-night binges of cookies and ice cream. If your goal is to pay off your car, you will have to get a handle on impulse spending. Keep your eyes on the prize, not the price.

A lack of purity can keep a person from their destiny. Everyone has seen this happen, especially in the age of no secrets. The gifted musician who can't control their urges, the phenom athlete who's running around on their spouse. I didn't want to jeopardize my ability to influence others or miss what God had for me over some reckless mistake. Like a pastor once said, "I don't fall off cliffs, because I don't go near them."

So, I resolved not even to kiss a girl until our wedding day.

That message does not go over well when you're trying to date. Even with girls from church. If any chemistry ever stirred up between me and a girl, I would have to let her know.

"I'm going to wait until I'm married."

"To have sex?"

"No," I would reply. "I'm not even going to kiss."

That'll turn things chilly really quick. *Gotta go. See ya, Darts!*

Was it frustrating? Sure. Especially once those birthdays started passing by. Nineteen, twenty-two, twenty-six . . . I'd never even had a girlfriend before.

Give Steve a Chance

*But whoever has this world's goods, and sees his brother
in need, and shuts up his heart from him, how does
the love of God abide in him?*

—I JOHN 3:17

You should get out and walk more. Seriously, like, right
now. Put the book down and take a walk. A short walk,
ten or fifteen minutes, is fine. Let your brain rest. Don't
look at your phone. Watch people. Pray and give thanks.
Often, I find the person God wants me to help when I'm
out walking around.

I was taking a stroll through my neighborhood one
afternoon when I saw a white-haired man in front of the
locksmith / taco shop / liquor store strip mall. He was
super thin and stooped over with a backpack on and some
clothes stacked on the curb. "How you doin' today, sir?"
I asked.

"I'm all right," he replied in a tired voice.

I introduced myself and he told me his name was
Steve. He was a sixty-seven-year-old veteran trying to

make it on the streets. "How long have you been out here?" I asked.

Steve stared blankly at the sidewalk. "Long time," he said.

We kept talking and I figured out that Steve was really just this cool older dude who'd been through a lot of hard things. Substance abuse, financial problems, relationship trouble, living on the streets. It made me wonder, could I end up homeless too? If so, what would I need? Food, medical care, money for basic needs.

After talking to Steve and hearing everything he was going through, it seemed like too big of a task for me. As much as I wanted to help, I knew he needed a lot more than I could offer. I was about to move on when I heard a familiar voice. *Ask him his bucket list,* God said.

"Got anything left on your bucket list?" I asked.

Steve lit up. "Yeah!" he said. "I'd like to go shark fishing, jump out of an airplane, and ride in a hot-air balloon."

"I can take you up in a balloon tomorrow morning," I told him. "How's five-thirty?"

"What?" he said. "Huh?"

"Just let me run and grab my stuff. I'll be back in a couple of hours. Be ready."

Steve raised one eyebrow like he didn't believe me, like maybe he had heard too many empty promises in his life. You should've seen his face when I showed up again with my backpack and keys to adjoining hotel rooms.

"Hang on," Steve said. "For real?"

We woke up at daybreak to board the giant multicolored balloon. It floated so high we could see the land spread out before us: tennis courts and swimming pools, vineyards, and rolling hills stretching to the ocean.

Steve shook his head. "Beautiful," he said as the sun broke over the mountains. "Just look at it. No worries up here. I don't really have anything that compares to this. Thank you, Jimmy. This might be the most amazing thing I've ever done."

"So, you'd consider adopting me?" I asked.

"Absolutely," he said.

The balloon pilot brought us safely to the ground. On the ride back into town, I asked Steve how he felt. "Mixed emotions," he confessed. "I'll remember this day for the rest of my life, but I know what's waiting for me when I get back on the streets. That kind of freedom ain't there. It'll be back to the responsibilities of life and everything that comes with it."

We rode without talking, letting it sink in. I didn't know if any of this would make a difference once Steve was back on the street. He'd never forget that moment in the balloon—that's worth something—but I didn't want it to be the only dream he checked off. I broke the silence to ask Steve an important question. "You ready to catch that shark?"

"You serious, Jimmy?" he said.

A few days later, our chartered boat slammed against the waves, dolphins gliding alongside and sea lions barking as we passed the buoys. "Always dreamed of reeling in a shark," Steve told me. "But I never thought I'd really be out here. Think we might see a hammerhead?"

The closest Steve got to a shark was a four-inch surf-perch, but we had a good time. Steve was easygoing, funny, cracking up our captain and crew. Everybody liked him.

Sailing back to shore, Steve started to open up, talking about his struggles with depression and chronic pain. The pain led to drugs and drugs just caused more sickness and hurt. "I was in the hospital for eight months," he said. "Got down to a hundred and sixteen pounds. I lost my home, my truck, a good job. I lost everything."

Steve didn't tell us all that to get sympathy. He was simply sharing his story with a few new friends. "I'm just trying to save up and get my own place again so I can live out the rest of my life in peace."

The boat pulled into dock. I dropped Steve off at his motel. "Sorry you didn't catch a shark," I said.

Steve laughed. "Ah, that's okay." He slid his skinny arm around my shoulder and told me how much the day had meant, how he hadn't felt that good in a long time.

"Hey, Steve?" I said before we went our separate ways.

"Yeah?"

"When's the last time you were in an airplane?"

I've got a picture on my phone of Steve jumping out of that plane, eyes bugged out and a smile billowed by a mouthful of wind, looking so different from the tired old man I'd met a few days before. At that moment, Steve looked like a kid on Space Mountain.

"Jimmy," he said after he'd kissed the ground. "No doubt, this is the best day of my life."

Six thousand dollars was raised for Steve after the video of his bucket list adventure went viral. We helped him get into a small apartment and connect with a local church that would love on him and point him to the resources he'd need to stay off the streets. The rest was between God and Steve.

About six months later, I pulled into a parking lot and spotted Steve. This time, he wasn't stooped over or looking lost. He'd gained some weight and was driving a tan Chevy Blazer.

I called out to him. "Steve?"

"Yeah," he laughed. "I got myself a car."

"That's awesome," I said.

"Hey, I got to go to the Angels game a few days ago," Steve said. "That was on my bucket list too."

"Sounds like you're doing pretty good."

"Doing all right," he replied. "One day at a time."

. . .

You don't have to put yourself in danger on the streets or spend a lot of money making a stranger's bucket list come true. Just go outside, look up from your phone, and pay attention. Buy a coffee for the person behind you in line. See that senior citizen eating by themselves? Find the waitstaff and pay for their meal.

It doesn't even have to be a stranger. A co-worker, classmate. Even an enemy. I believe you will never go broke by giving.

Ask God to show you how to help. Understand that it may not be the most obvious person. You might walk past someone on crutches to bless the guy driving a Lexus because, spiritually, he's the one who needs it most. Everybody's struggling with something.

If you find yourself face-to-face with a huge tattooed guy, just remember he used to be a tiny baby you could hold. If you're talking with someone who seems intimidating or mean, remember they were once a five-year-old getting picked last at gym class for a team. Picture people as kids and it helps you look past the surface and see their humanity. And when you find that shared space of humanity, you can help turn around the most hopeless, awful, discouraging day with a kind word, a laugh, or some small act of generosity.

The world desperately needs people who love others as radically as God does. No matter what they believe or what they have done, love can break the hardest heart. That's not just my optimism or opinion. Jesus said that you can't tell who's real by the causes they endorse or what kind of church they attend. The true followers of God are marked by a love that knows no bounds, constantly received and freely given, for the source of this love is infinite.

Stranger, neighbor, enemy, or friend—whose life can you change today through the power of love and kindness?

The Lights Are Green

But those who wait on the LORD shall renew their strength;
they shall mount up with wings like eagles, they shall run and
not be weary, they shall walk and not faint.

—ISAIAH 40:31

In spring 2022, I was asked to speak at a giant youth conference called The Send in Kansas City. The event was to be held in Missouri's mammoth Arrowhead Stadium, home of the NFL's Chiefs. I was excited to share the platform with speakers I admired, such as Lou Engle and Francis Chan. Then the organizers explained that I would actually be talking at an afternoon youth group meeting with a few other Christian influencers at a small church down the road from the big event.

I didn't want to go all the way to the smack-dab center of America to teach some church how TikTok works. But a voice pinged in the back of my head, reminding me that when opportunities land in my lap out of nowhere, they're usually from God. They may not be the most glamorous opportunities, but it's usually at the humble, simple ones where something amazing happens.

I jumped into the car with my friend Gabe, and we headed east. On the way, I began to get excited about what the Lord might have waiting, joking around, saying things like "Oh, maybe my future wife will be there!" (LOL, young single Christians think this before any church event.)

We arrived late and slipped into a back pew. There might have been a couple of hundred people there. A girl was sitting several rows up. Long black curls spilled over her shoulders. I was like, *Oh my goodness, wow, her hair is beautiful.*

She turned, and I caught a glimpse of her face. There was something about her. She looked lively and full of joy and kind and . . . I don't know how to explain it. Something! Like, something so powerful that I shut my eyes and said,

Jesus, please let me marry that girl.

I would have to find a way to meet her first. I'm not the kind of person who comes in hot and flirty. I grew up with two sisters. I'm not going to swarm over a girl like some creep.

Eventually, it was my turn to speak as part of the panel on Influence and Culture for the Kingdom.

I began to talk about green light Christianity. Most Christians were living red light Christianity, meaning they wouldn't take action or chase their dreams unless they had millions of signs to do it and even then would still be anxious to step out when God already said, "Go out in the world and share the Gospel." He already gave us a green light, so go accomplish what lies before you until He gives you a red light. Start with a green light. The church has massive purpose but little drive. The world has massive drive but little purpose. But when you can combine the two, something powerful can happen.

When I finished speaking, the service was nearly over. The guy in charge said, "Brother Jimmy, do you want to pray before we close?"

"Sure," I replied. "Okay."

After the event, everyone was out in the foyer, talking and milling around. I paced the edge of the room, trying to linger, hoping I'd run into the girl with the long curly hair. (Yes, even after I prayed to live like the lights were green. Maybe that word was for me?)

Sure enough, we met at the doorway.

"Hi," she said.

"Hey," I replied.

If we were making a movie of this, the awkward silence would be really cute. At the time, it just felt awkward. "My name's Jimmy," I said.

"Mariana," she replied.

She had a guy friend with her and I wasn't sure what the relationship might be, so I tried to be cool. His name turned out to be Jimmy too. To be safe, I talked to them both.

"Where are you guys from?" I asked.

"Palm Springs," Mariana said.

"Palm Springs? That's my favorite place in the world! I grew up visiting my grandparents there. Where I live now is like, less than two hours away." *Confirmation! The light is green!*

We kept talking until my friend yelled my name loudly enough to get my attention. He'd been trying for some time, but I must have been mesmerized by those curls and her eyes and dazzling smile and . . . oh, yeah, the other Jimmy.

"Ohh, I gotta jet," I told them. "Hey, can I get both y'all's numbers? I'd love to stay connected." (Other Jimmy, if you're out there, sorry, brotha. I was really only interested in connecting with her.)

My friend gave me a hard time in the car. "You like that girl a lot, don't you?"

It's a good thing I was in the back seat of the car so he

couldn't see how red my face had turned. "Oh, yeah," I replied casually. "She's pretty cool."

Inside, my heart was lit up and bouncing off the walls of my chest. *Is this it, Jesus? Finally?*

What if I never see her again?

Hell's Scared

And the LORD God said, "It is not good that man should be
alone; I will make him a helper comparable to him."

—GENESIS 2:18

That night, a second event for Kansas City's The Send
was held in a big church tent. I caught a glimpse of Mariana and made my way over through the crowd. This
time, Other Jimmy wasn't around.

We picked right up where we left off. The conversation flowed, with us laughing and teasing each other a
bit. It was one of those times when you feel like five
minutes have passed, but when you look, it's been two
hours. I offered Mariana a ride back to the Airbnb where
she was staying.

"Oh, um, okay," she said. "You sure?"

"Yeah," I told her. "Don't worry, I got it."

On the way, we passed this beautiful bridge over the
highway that was all lit up at night. "That bridge is so

candy," I told Mariana. "Are you in a hurry to get back, or . . . ?"

"No hurry," she said. "We can stop."

I parked and we made our way out. The bridge is a very romantic spot. Mariana and I stood at the rail, looking over the downtown skyline. "I need to tell you something," I said.

"Sure. Go ahead."

"I don't want to kiss someone until I marry them."

She stared up at me with those big brown eyes, slightly smiling like she knew some secret that she wasn't telling yet. This is usually where I'd get a reply like *Oh. That's nice. No, really, good for you* . . . while any attraction that had been there before disappeared. But Mariana kept smiling.

"I love it," she said. "That's what I've always wanted to do as well."

We snapped a selfie on the bridge to remember the moment and then I dropped Mariana off at her Airbnb. She shut the door behind her and, with a dazed look, informed her roommates, "Oh my gosh. I think I just met my future husband."

But I wouldn't know that for a long time.

•   •   •

I made Mariana's Instagram pic the wallpaper on my phone before I left the Midwest. It felt good knowing that she was headed the same direction on her way back home. Two people from Southern California meet fifteen hundred miles away in a small Kansas City church? What are the odds?

She wanted to drive to where I lived to go to a worship concert, but her car broke down so I ended up driving two hours to Palm Springs to pick her up for our first official date. I wanted to take her to the nicest restaurant I could, so we went to the Ritz-Carlton on the top of the mountain there. You know that feeling when you're with someone and it's just easy? You don't have to be careful about what you say or act like something that you're not. That's the kind of peace I felt with her.

I told Mariana all my hopes and dreams that night, about the television show and giving away millions and that I might even feel led to go into politics someday. She didn't roll her eyes and say "Ha, ha, Jimmy! You're so crazy!" Instead, she listened and was supportive of everything. I'd never felt that sort of affirmation from a person outside of my family. A lot of times, people think I'm unrealistically optimistic.

So, I popped the question right there at the Ritz-Carlton overlooking Frank Sinatra Drive. No, not *that* question. "Do you want to be my girlfriend?" I said.

"Yes."

"Then can I hold your hand?"

Big smile, brighter than the Palm Springs lights. "No," she said. "Not yet." Then I realized she was the right one. I found out that she was more sold out than me.

After dinner, we were standing out front by the Ritz-Carlton's fountain. A man walked by wearing expensive clothes, clearly one of the wealthy people staying at the hotel.

"Hey, I'll give you five hundred bucks to stand on top of the fountain and belly-flop into it," I said.

And he did! Water splashed everywhere and Mariana looked at me like, *Who the heck is this guy, and how does he get people to do all this crazy stuff?*

.   .   .

After spending five hundred dollars on the Ritz-Carlton belly flop, the only place I could afford to stay was the Palm Springs Motel 6. I slept there for the next few days while courting Mariana and getting to know her folks. One night, she tagged along with me to Walmart so I could show her what I did every day. I was a little apprehensive, even though I wanted to show Mariana how making undercover kindness videos worked. Taking people on challenges can be tricky. They mean well and want to help but end up complicating things by blocking the shot or pulling the focus away from a key moment.

We spotted this precious lady near the self-checkouts wearing leopard-print pants and a matching bandanna. Wavy white hair stuck up from the top of her bandanna with a long brown ponytail falling over her shoulder from below. She looked like the happiest person in the world.

"Okay, *her,*" Mariana said with an elbow to my ribs. "She's gotta be the one."

We said a quick prayer for confirmation. I felt peace, like *yep, go ahead.*

I eased around a rack of sunscreen so I could approach the woman from the side. "I love your bandanna!" I told her. (First, the challenge.)

"Thank you!" she replied cheerfully.

"Do you think there's any way I could have it?"

"Oh, I would give it to you in a minute, honey," she explained. "But I had chemotherapy and my hairpiece would fall off."

"Really? Oh, I'm so sorry," I said. Mariana nodded along. I felt terrible for asking after that.

The lady waved off our sympathy with a laugh. "I lost both of my breasts to cancer and I own it," she declared. "I never lost my joy."

When a stranger tells you something like that, the challenge is off. I just straight up handed her five hundred bucks. "This will be for my grandkids," she said, holding back tears.

The posted clip ended up being only forty-four seconds, but we visited longer. Mariana was able to minister and pray with the woman in a way that, as a man, I would've never been able to do. It's like she knew the right questions to ask and things to say.

There was a sweet spirit in those moments, like Jesus met us right there between the cash registers and an endcap of two-dollar flip-flops. I'd shot hundreds of videos, but that one was like nothing I'd ever done before. It's like you did something that caused God to say *Good job, kid,* and that is the most amazing feeling in the world.

Mariana and I got back in the car. The experience was so powerful that we sat there for several minutes without speaking, staring through the windshield at the setting sun.

Mariana turned to face me. "Hell is scared of us," she said, "because of what we can do for the Kingdom of God."

I'm not a person who cries a lot. But that evening, sitting in the Walmart parking lot, I broke down. She was right. After so many years of praying and waiting, I finally had someone by my side.

Lil' Bit of Heaven Broke Loose

If you have a reason not to be like Him,
that's deception.

—DAN MOHLER

My best friend Ray and I were back home in Minnesota, sitting at my parents' kitchen island, bored on a summer Sunday night. "Hey, check this out," he said. "You know what tomorrow is?"

"Monday?" I replied.

"Yeah, but you know what else?"

I shook my head.

"July the eleventh," Ray said. "It's seven eleven, man."

"Whoa, you're right," I said, checking the calendar on the side of our fridge.

Social media is a fire that constantly needs fresh fuel to burn. I'm always trying to come up with new ideas and twists, things that haven't been done before. "You know what would be so sick?" I said. "What if we went to

7-Eleven tomorrow and gave everybody in the store seven hundred and eleven dollars?"

"Ya, bro, for sure." Ray nodded. "At exactly 7:11 P. M."

Some ideas come together just that fast. But was it a good one? "Minnesota's got 7-Eleven?" said Ray.

"I think so? Hey, Siri, what's the closest 7-Eleven to here?" I asked.

"The closest. 7-Eleven store. Is in Madison. Wisconsin," Siri replied. Hmm, not what I was hoping for.

Ray tilted his head, looking confused. "Hey, Siri," I said. "How long would it take to drive to Madison, Wisconsin, from Walker, Minnesota?"

Siri paused to think. Or she might've just wanted to throw a little tension in there before she dropped the bomb. "Traffic to Madison. Wisconsin. From Walker. Minnesota. Is light," Siri replied in her most professional tone. "And by my estimations. Should take. Approximately six hours and fifty-eight minutes. Via I-94 East."

Ray and I exchanged looks. Were we going to let a five-hundred-mile road trip stand in the way of a giveaway that cool—$711 at 7-Eleven on 7/11 at 7:11? It would be a *whole year* before we'd get a chance to do that again.

The next day, Ray and I jumped into my Honda and booked it straight down through Brainerd to Blaine, into

Minneapolis, and out the other side. We took the interstate until the big WELCOME TO MADISON sign came
into view.

We entered the city limits at twenty minutes to seven.
A Google Maps search showed me there were three
7-Elevens in Madison. "We gotta dial this in," I told Ray.
"I can't be handing out the money at 7:10 or 7:12. It has
to be exactly 7:11 P.M."

Ray and I walked into the first 7-Eleven, which was
located in an old office building on a busy street downtown. The aisles were tight and shelves tall, making the
store feel cramped even though we were the only customers inside. Grubby plexiglass surrounded the front counter
and the clerk had a face mask pulled up under his eyes.

I motioned to Ray. "Let's get outta here. The vibe's all
weird in this place. Besides, there's nobody here to give
any money to anyway."

We dashed to the next location, a few miles down the
road near the University of Wisconsin. To its credit, at
least it looked like a traditional 7-Eleven. But this one
had the opposite problem as the first store: it was too full.
Even in the middle of summer, there were a lot of college
students hanging around.

Some of the money I give away comes from dona-
tions, but this one wasn't a kindness test, so it was all out
of my pocket. I couldn't afford to give $711 to twenty

college kids. Who knows how many more would rush in after word of the initial exchange was blasted out?

At 6:55, I was in a panic, worrying that we'd driven seven hours just to strike out. We had one last 7-Eleven and sixteen minutes to get there. Ray bumped his fist against my dash. "Let's go, bro," he said.

Ray and I whipped into the parking lot of Madison's last 7-Eleven at 7:09 P.M. It was a working-class part of town, with people streaming in and out of the store, paying for gas, buying milk and diapers and big cans of Arizona iced tea. The clerk was joking around with customers like it was a neighborhood hangout where everybody knew one another. Lively, but not too busy. Good feel. Just right.

My phone flipped from 7:10 to 7:11. I walked inside and up to the counter. The clerk was as tall as me, with a mustache, dark glasses, and short braids with silver tips. "What's up, G?" he said. "Can I help you?"

I fanned out seven Ben Franklins with eleven singles on top. "I got seven hundred and eleven dollars for you," I told him.

"Me?" he asked, pointing to his chest, completely flabbergasted.

I pressed the money into his hand. "There you go." He reeled back, staring at the bills in disbelief.

A man wearing a blue work shirt was watching from

the other side of the register. I turned and handed him a stack of cash too. "What?" he said, one hand to his head, staggering. "Whaaaat?"

Another shopper rounded the aisle, drinking a peach Slurpee and trying to figure out what all the fuss was about. "It's 7:11 in 7-Eleven on 7/11," I said, holding out seven hundred and eleven dollars. "So, this is for you."

She nearly spit Slurpee all over me.

Just then, a slim guy in a Captain America tee came in, looking around like maybe it was a robbery or someone had choked on a roller dog. I checked my phone. Still 7:11. I met him at the door and gave him seven hundred and eleven dollars as well.

"Are you for real?" he said, looking at the bills, mouth open.

"Here you go, bro!"

Boom. Just that quick, the atmosphere turned surreal, like somebody had lit a string of five thousand firecrackers. The chain reaction shot us all into some crazy, surprise game show where money falls out of the sky. The clerk jumped over the counter and ran outside and somebody else was shouting and jumping up and down and there was laughing and hugs and people crying "Whaaat?" and "For real?"

An orange-wigged woman in blue polka-dot pants walked into the commotion. Someone tried to explain.

"As soon as the clock hit 7:11, dude come in giving everybody seven hundred and eleven dollars!"

"Whaaaat?" she cried.

But by the time she made it inside, it was 7:12. "Hey, it was my birthday today," Slim Captain America Guy told the woman. "Here, let me bless you."

"Ohh, baby!" I said as he handed over some of his cash. Everybody started dancing and clapping and when customers walked in too late for the money, the others would rush to the register and pay for their stuff. "You don't know how much we needed this," one lady told me, weeping and squeezing my hands. "You gotta come to my house and let me cook y'all dinner."

"Aw, thanks, but we're probably gonna need to head back."

"Where you from?" she asked.

"Walker, Minnesota," I said. "We drove all day just to get here."

"Here?" she said. "All the way from Minnesota?"

I've done hundreds of videos, and that part never gets old. When the spirit of joy and generosity hits and every person's feeling the love, like we really are all in this together down here. A little bit of heaven broke loose in that Wisconsin 7-Eleven on a summer night.

Ray and I got a motel room nearby, watching as the clip went viral and comments started pouring in.

No one talking about the guy instantly paying it forward, being nice is infectious JHALL

The people that walk in at 7:12 😵 LEX

I'm not crying. you are TIFFANY EDGAR309

Even 7-Eleven's home office took notice, thanking us for the free commercial, clicking like, and following my channel.

There was one last bit of serendipity. After we got home to Walker, Ray gave me a funny look. "Hey," he said. "You'll never guess how long the trip back took."

I shook my head, laughing. "Bet I can guess."

.   .   .

There was no altar call at the end of that video. I didn't jump in with a Scripture reference or devotional thought. And yet, the love of God was all over it, as powerful and real as that moment in the store.

When I shoot a challenge, I always remind people that Jesus loves them and wants good things for their lives. Usually, I leave those parts out. My concern is that the algorithms will ban or reduce the reach of a video that mentions Jesus, which would also decrease the amount we could raise to help others.

A lot of people are turned off to church, preachers, and Christians. I don't want to leave those viewers out. I wouldn't want them to miss an opportunity to give or be inspired to help because of a negative experience with church somewhere in their past.

I've learned that you don't have to say the name of Jesus to love someone like Jesus. Check out 1 John 3:18 (NIV): "Dear children, let us not love with words or speech but with actions and in truth." Be thoughtful. Be sensitive. Be kind. When it comes to witness, words are overrated. Let your actions speak. Represent God with excellence and heart.

One of the most dangerous quotes of all time is "Preach the Gospel; use words if necessary." The idea is to let your life preach the Word and not rely on words, but the spoken Word of God—actually saying the name of Jesus—is so powerful. A lot of people have taken that quote to live lukewarm lives, saying: "Brother, I don't talk about Jesus or tell anyone. I just try to live and do good."

But the truth is, you could live perfectly and people still aren't going to be saved by just your actions. Words are necessary too.

VI

What the Heck

See Everything Happy

You can never outgive God.

—AS HEARD FROM DON JAMES

I flew out to Nashville to meet with a writer and brainstorm the making of this book. While praying, I mentioned Chuck E. Cheese, and when I finished, he told me that as a teen, he'd spent some time in the costume of the world's second most famous mouse. That's right. Charles Entertainment Cheese.

I almost fell out of my chair, like John the Revelator seeing a golden city come down from heaven. For me, it was a full-on confirmation from God.

"Whatever else happens, we gotta put that in the book," I told him.

"Put what in?" he said.

I guess I thought professional writers would be college professors or serious book people types. Maybe most of them are, but God sends me the one writer who's played Chuck E. Cheese? I've seen a lot of signs and wonders in my life. That ranks up there with the best.

I needed to shoot a video, so he drove me to a part of Nashville with a bunch of run-down houses and stores with security bars on the windows right next to a row of those skinny cube-shaped condos. It was a clear spring day and it seemed like the entire neighborhood was outside, riding bikes, sitting on porches, and hanging out on street corners to talk.

We were driving slow, arms out the windows. "Jimmy Darts!" some kid on a rent-a-scooter cried out. Guess he'd seen my videos.

"So, how do you know the right person to help?" Formerly Chuck E. asked. "Does God show you somebody or talk to you or something?"

"It's hard to explain," I said. "Usually, it just happens."

"Hope I get to see it," he said.

We parked at the Piggly Wiggly and walked around. I met some nice people but didn't get any nudges. Next, we went downtown and talked with some of the folks who sell a newspaper for the homeless. Still nothing. Then we got thrown out of the children's library because we were talking about how books work and I got too loud. After that, we decided to call it a day.

"Sorry you didn't see anything," I told Chuck E. as we steered back onto the interstate.

"Ah, that's okay," he said. "I guess you can't force these things."

·   ·   ·

The next day, we were driving around a little town out east of Nashville, telling stories for the book. I'd forgotten about filming any videos. We were sitting at a red light when I noticed a sky-blue thrift shop next to the county jail.

"Look at all that cool junk out front," I said, pointing to a mannequin in a cowboy hat next to some wheel-chairs and a three-legged pinball machine. "Man, I love thrift stores."

"Me too. You wanna check it out?"

The place smelled like old clothes and stinky feet inside. Everything was dirt cheap: cushy gold sofas and recliners with duct tape on the seat, plaques with inspira-tional sayings, and pictures of the Last Supper. There was a pile of raggedy sneakers for, like, fifty cents a pair.

A giant man, well over six feet tall, stood at the regis-ter, speaking to the cashier in what sounded like Spanish. He was rugged-looking, like a lumberjack or someone who wrestles bears for fun. The man was holding a Bar-bie, and in his shopping cart sat the tiniest, cutest dog in the world. I had an idea.

Propped in the corner was a collection of used

crutches. I grabbed one and took it to the counter where the big man was standing, making sure to limp a little as I walked up to him.

"Excuse me, sir?" I began. "These crutches are two dollars and I was wondering if you could help me out with a dollar or something?"

The big man pointed to me. "*No!*" I made a quick check of the distance to the exit. "I pay *two* dollars for you!" he said.

He motioned to the crutches. "Put it on my tab," he told the cashier. "I pay."

"Oh, thank you," I replied. "My knee is bad and I've been having a hard time getting around."

"Is okay, my man. You see the wheelchairs out front? I don't mind buying you one if you need it."

"No, no. This is more than enough." I reached to shake his hand. "What's your name?"

"Cruz."

"I'm Jimmy," I said. "Why did you help me?"

"I'm from Honduras, find happiness." Cruz paused, searching for the correct translation until he finally motioned around him to the clerks and the crutches and even the stinky pile of shoes. "See *everything* happy!"

"You've got so much joy," I told him. "It's contagious."

"Oh, I'm so happy!" he replied. "With two dollars! Two dollars makes a difference, you know?"

One aisle over, Chuck E. was pretending to browse used XXL nightgowns, eyes wide, watching the whole thing unfold as Cruz told me he'd been talking to the thrift store about buying some of their crutches and wheelchairs to send to the needy back home. It was like we'd hit a kindness challenge jackpot.

"I got something for you," I said, gladly handing over a stack of twenties. "Five hundred dollars."

"Ah-ah!" Cruz said, waving the money away. "Why you do that?"

"Because you were willing to help me!"

The cashier started clanking a cowbell while another worker let out a whoop. Chuck E. joined us up front, introducing himself.

Once things calmed down, I asked Cruz, "Is there anything I can pray for you about?"

A young man, early twenties maybe, had been standing silently off to the side. Cruz spoke to him in Spanish, waving him closer. "This is my son, Melvin," he told us. "He got in a car accident eight years ago back in Honduras."

Cruz's son hobbled over, leaning against the cart to pull up the leg of his pants. From the knee down was swollen, red, covered with jagged white scars, and so mangled that it looked like the bone was about to stick through his skin.

We laid hands on his leg and began to pray. It wasn't a Pentecostal, Baptist, Catholic, or Charismatic kind of prayer. It was just one of those heartbreaking, call-out-for-God-to-help-good-people-who-are-struggling kind of prayers. Even the puppy got a paw in on it. (Seriously. Watch the video.)

"That prayer made my day," Mr. Cruz said, wiping away tears. "All I want to see is my son to walk better."

We wiped out the thrift shop's inventory of crutches and wheelchairs for Cruz to send back to Honduras. After a few more hugs and handshakes, we headed back out to the car.

"You wanted to see it in action," I told Chuck E. "That's one of the kindest people I've ever met. I bet heaven is going bananas right now, so excited to see his life changed. No way I could've picked or found that guy. That was straight up Jesus right there."

At that moment, Cruz and his son walked out the front door with the crutches I'd asked him to buy for me. They didn't see us sitting in the car. He raised his hands to heaven and gave thanks to God. Then he put his arm around his son and they fell on each other and cried.

.   .   .

I set up a GoFundMe to help Cruz's son have surgery on his leg. Over fifty thousand dollars came in overnight.

We drove out to the little tire shop where Cruz and Melvin worked.

"Hey!" Cruz greeted us. "My friend, Jimmy!"

"Hey, brother! Where's your son?"

From the corner of my eye, I saw movement beneath a nearby jacked-up truck. Melvin crawled out, shook the dirt off his clothes, and limped over to where we stood.

"You crawl under cars?" Chuck E. asked.

"Working," he replied with a smile.

I told them about the money that had come in. "Man, you got to be kidding me!" Cruz replied. "Really? It's going to be possible?"

It's always a shock that people give money to help someone they don't know, especially when they're struggling too. But I guess they feel like I did as a kid back in Minneapolis. Whether it's one dollar or one hundred dollars—that's just something God put inside each one of us: to find joy and fulfillment through caring for others. "Really," I promised. "You're going to be able to fix your son's leg."

That's where Cruz's video stopped, but his story had just begun. The doctor for the Nashville Predators hockey team saw the clip and called a colleague at Vanderbilt University Medical Center. That surgeon brought in a specialist. After X-rays and tests, the doctors discovered that Melvin needed both legs fixed. He'd been compensating with the other one for too long. The procedure would cost more than fifty thousand dollars, but Vanderbilt and the good people of Tennessee jumped in to make sure it happened.

Eight months later, I returned to Nashville to work on this book some more. A freak snowstorm shut the city down, but we took a break and drove over the ice to check on Cruz and Melvin. Cruz was out helping some stranded motorists, but Melvin was there, still working.

"How's your leg?" I asked.

A huge smile lit his face as he stood and walked over to us. We stared, mouths open, too amazed to speak. He wasn't limping. Not even a little.

Melvin tapped his phone, opened a translator app, and spoke Spanish into the mic. For some reason, the high-pitched voice of a little girl emerged. "No pain! Thank you so much. Thank you to all the people who helped me. Thanks to you, now I can walk again." Chuck E. and I looked at each other like *what?* We didn't know whether to shed tears from witnessing Melvin's miracle or bust out laughing at the way he'd told us through the voice of a little girl.

God lets me be the face of undercover kindness, but the most important work takes an army of support: single moms and truckers, surgeons and pro athletes, YouTube stars and missionaries, people who don't even believe.

That's how kindness works, overcoming doubts and fears and all the distance between us. It multiplies, overflowing into the lives of others until everybody has more than enough. And when a big, burly mechanic uses a little girl's voice to say thanks, it's all part of the fun.

Sunshine was turning the ice to slush as we slid back home. "Ever get used to it?" Chuck E. asked.

"Used to what?"

"Seeing miracles."

"Nah, man," I told him. "Joy never gets old. I'm gonna keep on doing this for as long as I can."

A Donkey, a Burning Bush, or Even Me?

A man's difficulty in stillness is in exact proportion
to his interest and attraction to things other
than or more than God's presence.

—ERIC GILMOUR

Remember the brief time I lived in Austin because I felt God told me to move there? It was a whirlwind—a season where every decision felt like a leap of faith. I was working as a waiter at the JW Marriott and struggling to make ends meet. But here's the kicker: I'd locked myself into a long-term lease in a luxury high-rise. It had a spiral staircase and incredible views, but my furniture? A blow-up bed on the floor.

I was in over my head financially, living way beyond the means of a waiter who largely works the breakfast shift. Most of my paycheck evaporated into rent. I'd come home each day exhausted after my shift and lie on my blow-up mattress staring at the fan on the vaulted ceiling, remembering how simple it was living back with ministry friends in Redding. It was then that I started consulting God on every decision, no matter how small. I wanted to invite Him into everything, even the small stuff, and fully embrace a life where faith—not just logic or personal comfort—led the way.

One day I was praying about where I should work out, and felt God leading me to Life Time fitness. I couldn't believe it. I could barely afford my rent—why was God telling me to go sign up for a gym with an expensive monthly fee? But He'd been clear, and if there's one thing I've learned, it's that God's plans often don't come with a budget-friendly guarantee. So, with a lump in my throat the size of Texas, I walked out of my apartment and straight through the doors of Life Time, where I signed a contract and prayed I wasn't making another huge mistake.

And that's when it happened.

Out of the corner of my eye, I saw Ryan Moran. Ryan was a prominent figure in the e-commerce world, known for his early success building Amazon businesses. I had spent hours consuming his YouTube content, trying to pick up his tactics and apply them to my own ventures. In fact, his advice had been the driving force behind my short-lived attempts to sell fidget spinners and my ill-fated No Mice! product. My first instinct was to run over and introduce myself. My second instinct was to run for the exit.

Before I could chicken out, I walked up and said, "Hey, Ryan. I'm Jimmy. Huge fan of your work. I've been trying to start some products of my own."

He looked up and smiled. "Thanks, man. You know, I'm actually putting on an event soon—Capitalism Conference. It's all about helping entrepreneurs scale their businesses and take things to the next level. You should check it out."

I couldn't believe it. Ryan Moran, someone whose work I'd admired for so long, was inviting me personally to attend his event. It felt surreal, getting direct validation from someone I'd looked up to for years. But when I got home and checked the details, the excitement quickly faded. Tickets were $1,200. That alone was a gut punch.

As I scrolled further down the website, still lying on my partially deflated blow-up bed, I saw the event location: the JW Marriott in downtown Austin. The same place I spent my days working to barely make rent. I couldn't believe it. I didn't need $1,200 to get into the room—I just needed an apron and a shift on the floor. I ended up working that shift and had a number of the attendees eat at the restaurant. In between serving, I'd pick their brains. I learned a ton and became encouraged after my No Mice! misadventure. Shortly after, I launched on Amazon with CLOSED FOR CLEANING signs—that brought in three to four thousand per month. This provided me the freedom to travel and begin making videos full-time. Fast-forward a few years. By then I'd built a career traveling the country, making videos, and helping people—and the dream of my making it big selling on Amazon had mostly faded but I had the freedom to pursue my true passion. One day I was fundraising on a live stream upstairs at my parents' house in Minnesota when a donation popped up: Ryan Daniel Moran. My jaw hit the floor. I reached out to him immediately.

"Hey, is this *the* Ryan Moran?" Turns out, it was. Not only did he remember me, but he said he'd been following my work. Then he texted the words that stopped me in my tracks:

Jimmy, why don't you come speak at CapCon?

The conference I couldn't afford to attend? Now I was going to be onstage? It felt like a movie plot. But the night I arrived, God dropped something heavy on my heart. *Pray for healing during your speech,* He said. I groaned.

"God, this is a business conference, not a church service. Are You sure?" But I knew better than to argue. If He said to do it, I'd do it.

The next morning, I stepped onto the stage as the opening speaker. I told my story—how God had led me to Austin, how He'd connected the dots in ways I never could have imagined, and how faith had been the cornerstone of my journey. I could sense the crowd enjoyed my message, laughing at the punch lines and nodding in agreement to key takeaways. Toward the end, I took a deep breath and asked the audience, "Is anyone here dealing with pain or challenges? If so, raise your hand. I'd like to pray for you."

For a moment, the room was silent. Then, one by one, hands started going up. I prayed right there: for healing, for breakthroughs, for restoration. And then I asked, "If anyone just experienced something—a shift, a breakthrough, a healing—raise your hand again."

Hands shot up. One man who had come to the conference wearing a wrist brace shared that his wrist, which had been immobile for months, was suddenly fine. Another shared that he'd just received a text about a business deal he'd been agonizing over—it had gone through. And then there was the man who felt so stirred that he said he was going to pay off the mortgages for an entire street. The room buzzed with energy. In that moment, it felt less like a business conference and more like a revival.

Ryan, trying to temper the audience and re-command the room, said, "Well, that's not what I expected." It was as though he was trying to bring things back to center, but it was obvious the atmosphere had already shifted. Even in a room full of business-minded types—some of them very successful—there was no shortage of needs and anxieties.

Even Ryan's business partner, Matt, was moved. Earlier that day, Matt was dragging his feet just to get to the conference and didn't even want to attend. He later told me that during his Uber to the conference, as the car slowed to a crawl in traffic, he thought, *If this Uber comes to a full stop, I'm getting out and heading back.* That's how much he didn't want to be there. But something kept him on track. By the end of my talk, he was in tears.

Later, as I stood offstage with a long line of people waiting to connect with me, Matt approached. He shook my hand and shared how deeply my message had moved him. He told me he'd sold a business with Ryan a few years prior and had been sitting on the sidelines, longing to do something meaningful for God's Kingdom.

"Jimmy," he said, "you've inspired me. I'd be willing to work on anything with you—even for free. I just want to support what you're doing."

I was taken aback. Here was Matt, someone who had helped Ryan achieve such incredible success, offering to come alongside me—a guy who had failed on Amazon time and time again. But his generosity was overflowing, and it was clear he believed deeply in what I was saying. It was evident he felt he was meant to be there, to hear my story, and for us to connect.

That conversation led to OverFlo, a company dedicated to providing clean drinking water to families in need. The name itself came from the idea of overflowing generosity. For every bag of our hydration product sold, a family gets thirty days of clean water. It's a simple concept with a profound impact, but building it meant partnering with people who shared the same vision.

One of those people was Scott Harrison, the founder of Charity: Water. I first encountered Scott back in ministry school, where his personal testimony of being a nightclub promoter, which left him feeling empty, had ultimately translated into him creating one of the most successful nonprofits in the world. His organization had transformed millions of lives by providing access to clean water, and they were the perfect partner to help bring OverFlo to life. We decided to not just sell a hydration product but create a system that incorporates built-in giving through sales. We wanted to ensure we could provide funding to the most capable nonprofits working to solve this problem, and for me, Charity: Water's proven track record made them the perfect partner. We'll see how OverFlo does in the market, but regardless of its success, it stands as a powerful part of my testimony of how God works in my life.

Looking back, it's clear none of this was random. Every step—from moving to Austin, to meeting Ryan at the gym, to being invited to speak at the conference I once couldn't afford—was part of a bigger plan. And the lesson is this: when God says *move,* move. When He says *speak,* speak. Obedience opens doors we never even knew existed.

If we are willing, God can speak through a donkey, a burning bush, or . . . lol, even me.

Yes Is Yes Forever

I found the one I adore!

—SONG OF SOLOMON 3:4 (TPT)

I paid over a thousand dollars to clear the ice rink at Rockefeller Center for four minutes. It was Christmas in New York City, and a huge crowd was on hand that night, shoulder to shoulder on the ice, surrounding the rink, and watching from above.

Mariana glided gracefully around me while I wobbled, lurched, and grabbed her arms for balance. I can't ice-skate very well, but it worked out in my favor. She thought that was the reason I was so nervous that night.

We'd been dating for nearly a year and a half, taking things slow. Having adventures together, road trips and Walmarts, waterslides and dollar stores, blessing strangers and blessing one another. Still no kiss.

Our moment arrived. The DJ announced that everyone should make their way off the ice for a special couple skate. I was about to whisk Mariana away when this random guy approached.

"Hey, would you mind taking a picture of me and my girlfriend?" he said, handing Mariana his phone.

"Of course!" Mariana replied. She's nice like that.

Mariana took his phone, tapping the screen to bring the pair in focus. All of a sudden, the guy dropped down and held out a ring to his girl.

Oh, no. Are you kidding me?

Security came over to break it up, politely telling the couple they would have to move to the side. Mariana handed his phone back as she pulled me toward the exit. "No, no," I told her, pulling back. "Let's stay for a bit."

"What do you mean?" she asked.

"Well, I paid a little more so we could skate alone. We've got one whole song to ourselves."

"Wait, you did what?"

"I Will Follow You" began playing over Rockefeller Center's sound system. "That's our song!" Mariana cried.

I held her close, swaying as R & B crooner Toulouse testified that the tallest mountain or deepest ocean could not keep me away from my love. Wherever you go, I will follow. You are my destiny.

I stumbled to a stop, holding on to Mariana's hands. Thousands looked on as we stood beneath Prometheus and that towering Christmas tree. With a million twinkling lights of red and green around us, I turned to face mi amor. Mariana took a sharp breath, realizing what was about to take place.

"Jimmy—?"

I got down on one knee. Actually, I slipped on the ice and landed on my knee. Regardless, I ended up in the proper position.

Mariana slapped her hand over her mouth as I said those four life-changing words. "Will you marry me?"

I think they heard her scream all the way over on Long Island. "YES!"

And the crowd went wild . . .

We left Rockefeller Center for Central Park. A horse-drawn carriage was waiting. Snuggled together on that plush leather seat, we talked about our wedding day. Mr. and Mrs. Kellogg, or Mrs. Darts? Where should we honeymoon? And where are we going to live?

If your relationship is built on the right foundation, those details really don't matter much. I'd waited a long time, but I've never met anyone who regretted taking things slow. Your yes is a yes forever.

Then, with the snow falling all around, we stood up in that carriage and began to dance.

VII

That's Candy

Help You More Than It Hurts Me

Do not forget to do good and to share,
for with such sacrifices God is well pleased.

—HEBREWS 13:16

It's a long, strange road from Southern California to Las
Vegas.

Ghost towns and billboards for alien beef jerky, fifties
diners and dinosaurs, tourists taking selfies next to giant
stacks of stones painted Day-Glo purple and orange.

I almost hitchhiked for fun. Just to depend on the
kindness of strangers. Just because it's fun to live a little on
the edge, not knowing if I was gonna make it to Las Vegas
or heaven.

As I was driving, I thought back to the prophecy I got
in Bible college. "So saith the Lord . . ." Hannah began,
"you will have a television show one day."

That sounded so insane. If she had told me that someday I'd climb Mount Everest and do a backflip off the top,
I would've probably said something like, "Wow, okay,

that's shocking but definitely doable. I'm just gonna have to put in some work."

Backflipping off Mount Everest would be easier than getting a TV show. People try to crack that code for years and never make a dent. I could work at it, but something that miraculous would have to come from the hand of God.

Seven years after that prediction, I was on my way to Vegas to shoot footage for what could be the first episode of my television show. But we weren't going to some glitzed-out studio or shooting location. Instead, I was headed to the most dangerous street corner in America with a thousand dollars cash. I was going undercover to change a stranger's life.

God is so wild.

·   ·   ·

I was hanging out in front of Lucky's Gaming and Spirits under some scraggly palm trees and a banged-up dumpster with spray-painted gang tags and trash spilling onto the ground. A vape shop and Family Dollar discount store sat next door. In the distance, the Las Vegas Stratosphere shot up two thousand feet like a mirage while an enormous LED sphere hyped Superbowl LVIII.

There were no lights, hype, or grand hotels where I was standing, only a street lined with economy apartments, strip mall churches, and signs advertising one-penny slots. Good news, though, at least the corner was no longer America's number one location for shootings and stabbings. Somebody told me it was only the fourth most dangerous now.

Oh, boy, keep me safe, God, I prayed, eyeing the production truck parked across the street. *And keep the crew safe too, amen.*

When I started doing the kindness challenge five years ago, it was mostly just me and God. It was our thing, going into a city on a mission to make someone's day. Now, cameras, trucks, and a whole crew were on hand to help me film. I couldn't help but wonder if that would change the free-spirited, easygoing feel. Even a blessing can be bittersweet sometimes.

The door at Family Dollar flew open and a woman started booking it across the parking lot, carrying an armload of plastic sacks with paper towels inside. Her straight black hair was pulled back in a ponytail and she was casually dressed in a hoodie and stretch pants. She looked determined or anxious or worried—or maybe all three.

"Excuse me," I called. "Ma'am?"

She stopped and walked toward me.

"Sorry to bother you," I said. "I'm just trying to ask for a dollar to get the bus out of here. I don't know if you have anything, but . . ."

With no hesitation, she opened her purse. "It's not gonna hurt you?" I asked.

"It'll help you more than it hurts me," she replied, reaching into her wallet and handing me two dollars with a sympathetic look that said *Kid, get out of here while you can.*

"Thank you," I said. "What's your name?"

"Lulu."

Big dimples dotted her cheeks as she offered me a quick but genuine smile. Some teeth were broken and missing in the front. She covered her mouth with her hand.

"I'm Jimmy. Good to meet you," I said.

"Nice to meet you, Jimmy," Lulu said, shaking hands. "Why'd you help me out?"

"Because anytime you need help, if I have it and I can, I will." She shouldered her bags and turned to leave. "You have a wonderful day."

"Hey, Lulu." I handed back her dollar bills. "Here."

"But you just asked me for it?" she said.

I pulled a stack of cash from my pocket. "I wanna bless you with a thousand dollars for being so kind."

Suspicion flashed across her face. "No, you don't," Lulu said. "That's not true."

"Yes, it is. I was trying to find the first person to help me." I spread out the bills, showing her that it was real and not some trick or a money-drop scheme. "Here, take it so no one sees right now." This was not an area of town where you should be waving around a thousand bucks.

"Are you sure?" she said. "That's a lot of money."

By that time, Lulu was crying and I was crying. Maybe even God was crying because a street corner marked by crime and bloodshed suddenly became filled with peace.

Lulu hid the money in her purse and wiped her face with her sleeve.

"Is it going to help out?" I asked.

"Oh, man, it's gonna do more than that," Lulu said, pointing to the apartment complex next door. "I got five kids at home."

"Yeah?"

"Just going through a lot lately." She nodded first, then slowly shook her head. "Trying to find a job. It gets harder to maintain everyday life."

"What's the toughest part about getting a job?"

"I don't have the smile," she said. "When you got a messed-up smile, people think you're a drug addict and they won't hire you."

"What's your dream?" I asked.

Lulu looked down the street and laughed softly like maybe she'd stopped dreaming to keep from being let down. "To be stable with my kids," she said. "And make sure they have everything they need."

Lulu and I prayed and exchanged numbers. She hugged me, thanked me, and headed to tell her kids the good news. Once she was out of sight, I ran across the street and climbed into the production truck. The entire crew was crying. "Jimmy, that was amazing," one crew member said. "While you were praying for Lulu on the street, we were back here praying too."

.   .   .

Lulu's video got six million views. I started a GoFundMe and asked her to meet me in the same shopping center the following day.

"Over forty-two thousand dollars was donated to help you out," I told her.

She turned away, burying her face in her sleeve. "No way . . ." Lulu said, her voice cracking. "Forty?"

"Over forty. And it's still coming in. We're going to help you. You're gonna be able to get new teeth."

"I don't even know what to say," she said, rocking back and forth, hands over her eyes. "I don't even know."

Joy Is So Contagious

For we are God's fellow workers;
you are God's field, you are God's building.

—I CORINTHIANS 3:9

We put Lulu on a plane to Nashville. Jason Aldean and his wife met her there and set her up with a reconstructive dentist to get a brand-new smile. There were also offers to help with a job search and better housing options for Lulu and her kids back in Vegas. Last I heard, she was working and, best of all, had rededicated her life to God. If Lulu was willing to help me when she had nothing, I don't doubt she's reaching out now to help others too.

The hardest part of the kindness challenge is following up after the video and fundraiser are done. I've always tried to stay in touch and do what I can, but after hundreds of challenges, it's become too much for one person. So, yeah, it's nice to work with a crew that has experience with outreach and support. That seems to be the lesson from God lately. It's not supposed to be *me*. We work together down here.

Speaking of teamwork, here's how I got the opportunity to make a TV show. A few years back, a television producer saw some of my clips and reached out to do a video together. He kicked off our collaboration with a challenge. "Give a thousand dollars to the first person who says yes to paying it forward."

I roamed the Walmart parking lot with bouquets of mixed flowers. Got a few dirty looks and uneasy smiles. Most shoppers simply walked faster and avoided making eye contact with me.

God always has that one person though. A woman wearing glasses and a friendly smile was getting into a minivan. I held out the bouquet. "Don't worry, they're free," I assured her. "We're giving out flowers today. Just pay it forward if you can."

"Oh! Of course!"

She poured all the change from her console into my hands. I gave her a thousand dollars for being kind. Her jaw hit the floor. "Wait, *whaaat*? Are you serious?"

Her response was so wild that a crowd had gathered to see what was going on. Joy is so contagious. I think we hugged half of Walmart and all of an Olive Garden that afternoon.

Our video quickly captured millions of views and was

featured on *Access Hollywood*. "Okay, wow," the producer said afterward. "This needs to be a show."

We started talking about how we wanted to make a good, wholesome television series that not only entertained viewers but also inspired them to reach out with acts of kindness. Nothing preachy or uptight. Just a group of buddies going on adventures to help people.

And that's how I ended up on the rough side of Vegas praying for me and the film crew not to get shanked. After saying goodbye to Lulu, we loaded our gear and headed for the Strip to get ready for the most expensive ticket in town—Super Bowl LVIII. Not to celebrate, though. The next day, we were taking two special guests to the game as part of our video shoot too.

I was so excited I could hardly sleep that night. I dozed off just before disaster struck. At four A.M., the sink pipes burst and flooded the room, soaking all of our luggage. I kinda loved it. I always want to stay easygoing. It keeps me humble and helps me to help others. I threw on wet clothes and downed some coffee, and we hit the road to give a stranger the surprise of their life.

A community center and a local veterans' group had connected us with a pilot whose military career was cut short due to the effects of Parkinson's disease. We showed up at his front door with Super Bowl tickets for him and his son.

Before the main event, we stopped by the community center's pregame party to hand out hot meals to the less fortunate. Steelers All-Pro quarterback Russell Wilson was there as well as this famous pastor named Judah Smith and I got to meet them both. Eventually, it was time to head over to Allegiant Stadium.

The Super Bowl in Vegas was as extreme as one would expect. The Chiefs were on fire all night, battling to an overtime finish. There was a moment when I looked around at all the flash and fireworks, the stands packed with sixty-one thousand roaring fans while one hundred and twenty-plus million watched at home and everybody was hugging and cheering and laughing and losing their minds. It wasn't just the excitement of the game. It was the joy of being together and completely alive in the moment.

I was two weeks away from my twenty-eighth birthday. It felt like God was winking at me and reminding me of our conversation on the mountain when He told me He wanted me to go and make videos for Him. At the time, I was confused, but now it all made sense. Still, as incredible of an event as the Super Bowl might be, it was nothing compared to what was about to happen next.

Peaceful and Wild

> The Kingdom of Heaven can be illustrated by the story of
> a king who prepared a great wedding feast for his son.
>
> —MATTHEW 22:2 (NLT)

I was bawling before my groomsmen even came out.

The venue was Palm Springs perfect. Mountains rising behind a sky blue pool, each blade of grass immaculately manicured, and every design element modern, lush, and fiercely chic.

I stood waiting in a classic black tuxedo, legs shaking and tears streaming down my face, bracing for Mariana to change her mind and run. The bride's music would start and we'd all be standing there with hands folded, looking back at the doors and . . . nothing. I'd be left sweating in a cheap tux, forever waiting for the first kiss, for marriage, for a whole new chapter of life to begin.

A part of me still couldn't believe that this beautiful, fun young woman of God was going to walk down the aisle in a white dress and agree in front of a preacher to support, love, and live with me for the rest of my life.

For the rest of *our* lives.

My brothers-in-law, Walker and Ray, were up there waiting with me, while my sisters (both pregnant!) stood on the bridesmaids' side. Seated in the first rows were my parents, grandparents, and in-laws, the sleek white chairs behind them filled with extended family, friends, business partners, and even some people from my videos.

Dina and I met near Joshua Tree a few weeks before the wedding. She answered the kindness challenge by offering me money for shoes, even though her car had broken down and cash was tight. My viewers chipped in enough to help her fix her car and get caught up on bills. Not only did Dina make the drive to Palm Springs, but she also wore the coolest Paris fedora with a big flower on it. "My mother told me to always wear a hat to a wedding," she explained.

I looked out over each face in the crowd, thinking of the stories and adventures we'd shared. Everybody I loved was together in one place. It felt like a symbol of God, the church, heaven, and everything good. I believe that all of us exist because God wants a family. Even when we turned away, God sent Jesus to welcome us back into the family.

I thought about a lot of things while I was up there,

sweating and waiting and trying not to bite my nails. Finally, the patio doors opened. A vision in white appeared. My lip began to quiver. She moved slowly, gliding down the aisle toward me. Before my future bride even got close, I burst into tears again.

Mariana stood beside me. Pastor Mark opened his Bible and told us to join hands.

"Beloved, we are gathered here today . . ." he began.

We made a promise before God, exchanging rings and vows. During mine, I turned to our family and friends and said, "I can't believe she hasn't backed out." Everybody laughed. Pastor Mark pronounced us man and wife. And then, it was time.

Our first kiss. Ever.

. . .

The reception got a little out of control.

Jericho, Frankie, Gabe, and Josh—a few of my YouTuber friends—led the charge at the dance party: standing on each other's shoulders, falling face down toward the tile floor before being caught at the last minute. We made a human jump rope and then took turns throwing each other into the air. At one point, I saw my five-year-old nephew, Graham, go flying up toward the ceiling, laughing the whole time. (Okay, maybe I was the one who helped throw him.)

Me and my groomsmen lifted Mariana up on a chair and she chucked water bottles into the crowd while everyone was dancing to clean versions of hip-hop and lots of cool Spanish rap that I couldn't understand. A mosh pit broke out to Taylor Swift, everybody flinging themselves around and crashing into one another. I grabbed Big Johnny and ripped off his shirt, then he threw a cake in my face. I think everyone within ten feet of the dance floor got a minor concussion.

An elderly couple attended the reception, and my mom and dad saw them the next day, all bruised and bandaged. "You'll never guess what happened to us," my dad overheard them saying. "We were at a sober wedding last night, and that's how we got beat up."

·   ·   ·

I get asked so many times what that first kiss was like. "Peaceful and wild," I reply. Sounds crazy, I know. How can something be both peaceful and wild? That's the Kingdom of God. Righteousness is a straight up thrill with none of the regret.

I went into our first kiss as a boy and by the time we parted lips, I felt like a grown man. Friends want to know how my life is different now that I'm married. I still love the rush of adrenaline and I will always love to stir up fun. But I'm much calmer now.

Just Help One

Therefore, as the elect of God, holy and beloved, put on
tender mercies, kindness, humility, meekness, longsuffering;
bearing with one another, and forgiving one another . . .
But above all these things put on love, which is
the bond of perfection.

—COLOSSIANS 3:12–14

My life seems chaotic sometimes, making videos and surprising people all over the world. I'm trying to slow
down, go deeper, and work on things that will last, like
writing this book. Who knows, I might even do another
after this one is done.

It's late now and everything is quiet. I'm lying on the
couch with my hands behind my head, thinking about
everybody who's reading these words and praying for
each one of you.

There are a few more things I want to say. Others
spoke life into me along the way, and my mission is to
carry that on. Before we go, I want to speak life to you.

I'm sure some people will read these stories and think

of all the reasons they're disqualified from doing something great with their lives. Maybe you didn't grow up in a small town with loving and supportive parents. Texting family and friends back might be a struggle for you—forget about reaching out to strangers or building and managing an online presence. You might not see yourself as outgoing or funny or the creative type.

None of that matters. God is looking for individuals, not copies. You are not disqualified. Our Father has no favorites. We are all His favorite.

God needs nurses and schoolteachers and people who cut hair and do it with conviction. I believe that whatever God calls you to do should be a blast because you're living for an audience of one.

That doesn't mean there won't be difficult days. Whatever you do, you're going to face opposition. You will fail and you'll struggle with doubt. Failure and struggle are like God's college. That's how He teaches and shapes us into what we're supposed to be.

Even when I was waiting tables—even when I was *clearing* tables and washing dishes—I was living purposefully in that place because my purpose is to express love through my life, whether I'm rolling silverware or working in partnership with the NFL.

Circumstances may change, but that central purpose never will. Whether I have a billion followers or only one, the message remains. It was true before me, and it will still be true long after I'm gone. No matter what you believe or what you have done, I want to let you know that you are radically loved.

The biggest lie on earth is that you are alone. If you need a father, there's one out there for you. And if you need a friend, He's the best one that you'll ever have. There are so many good people in this world. I plan to meet a whole lot more and hopefully, someday, I'll get to meet you.

Every day we have a choice. Choose love. Choose kindness. Speak life. Change lives. I truly believe that the most fun we can have on this planet is to spread joy and kindness like a virus. If you want the craziest, most fun-filled adventure you could ever imagine, choose to follow Jesus.

Sure, I've made mistakes. But I do my best to bring it to the Lord as quickly as possible and get my heart right with Him.

I don't think I'll receive any trophies in heaven for doing this work. The Bible says if everyone knows, you've already received your reward. Generosity should be a way of life, so natural to us that we don't even think about it. It's uncomfortable when someone tries to tell me how much good I'm doing or that I'm changing the world. Thanks, but my ego doesn't need to hear that. My main focus is cultivating a lifestyle in private that's pleasing to God.

There's nothing special about me. God has called me to a life of undercover kindness, and it's no better or worse than being an operations manager or sandwich artist. The real undercover heroes are the ones who watch the videos and give sacrificially to help a stranger get much-needed surgery, transportation, or a place to live.

Maybe you don't help hundreds. Just help one. All you have to be willing to do is step out in faith and walk in love. Just a little can make all the difference in the world.

God calls us to encourage and change the world, no matter how small your world might be. Whether it's your community, your school or job, your neighborhood, or even just your home. We are all influencers. So, why not inspire the kind of revolution that's bigger than all the crazy stuff that tears us apart?

I want to see amazing signs and wonders, lives changed, and live-streamed miracles that no one can deny. Strangers blessed, adventures and new friends, old folks and little children laughing in wide-eyed surprise. Even if I never see those things in my lifetime, I won't quit. I don't care if the internet disappears and we go from TikTok back to hand-cranked radios. I'll still be finding people, telling them they're amazing, and spreading Christmas cheer, even if it's the middle of August. As long as I am able, every day. That's candy.

I'm excited to see where undercover kindness takes me next. I'm still coming up with fun new ideas. Dressing up like an old man and falling down to see who will help me back up . . . going door-to-door asking strangers if me and Ray can have my birthday party at their house . . .

Some worry that I don't offer enough sermon tie-ins or theological insights, but I think that might miss the point. Undercover kindness is spontaneous, stepping out with childlike faith. If I'm out on the streets looking sad, hungry, or desperate, I believe God will show up and send somebody to help. When we help each other, it's a sermon that goes beyond words.

They tell me books should have a theme. This is mine: Have fun with God and help everybody you can. Kindness can break the hardest heart.

Remember that God loves you for who you are and He thinks you're hilarious. And I love and appreciate every one of you.

You're amazing!

See What He Will Do

Nowhere in Scripture does Jesus say, "Pray this specific prayer, then live lukewarm, and you'll be saved." Instead, the Bible says, "Confess with your mouth and believe in your heart, and you will be saved" (see Romans 10:9). This wasn't meant to be done out of fear or just to avoid hell—it's about responding to a revelation of His love and a genuine desire to serve Him because of what He's done for you.

Think about it: if someone holds a door open for you, you say "Thank you." If a stranger buys you a meal anonymously, you're blown away. If someone pays off your mortgage, you weep with gratitude and invite them into your home.

Now imagine if someone died for you—not a friend or family member, but a stranger, even while you were living in ways completely opposed to them. You'd be so moved you'd say, "I'll live the rest of my life serving you!"

That's exactly what Jesus did for each of us. He died for us while we were still sinners. Without Jesus, without surrendering to Him, we're like children running from their Father. But He's inviting us to come close, to be His friend, and to let Him guide our lives. He wants to warn us of dangers we don't see, remove what doesn't belong in our lives, and lead us into His perfect plan—one full of love, joy, and purpose.

This surrender is about saying: Hey, God, You're right. I don't want to do this life alone, living like a child running my whole life away from You, my Father. I want to be close to You. I actually want to be Your friend. I want You to tell me when there's a trap ahead that I can't see. I want You to show me the things in my life that You never designed for me to carry—things the world might call moral or that pastors and other Christians might say are okay, but that You don't.

I want You to have the freedom to convict me, to close and open doors even when I don't understand. I want You to answer my prayers when it's right and to withhold answers when You know what's best for me in the long run. I trust You, Jesus, and I want to give my life to You—fully, not partially.

I repent for doing life my way. I repent for living by

what seems right to man, following my flesh instead of Your Spirit and the words in Your glorious love letter, the Bible—a guide to living life with You. Jesus, I believe You lived, I believe You died on the cross for my sins, and I accept You into my life to be the King of my heart. Holy Spirit, I invite You to move into me, to lead me, to teach me to love, and to convict me through this journey called life.

Help me to live a life full of adventure, free from fear, full of love, empty of selfishness, and overflowing with grace for others.

This is the call of salvation: to respond to Jesus with love, gratitude, and complete surrender—not out of fear, but out of a deep understanding of who He is and what He's done for you.

For we too once were foolish, disobedient, deceived, enslaved to various sinful desires and pleasures, spending and wasting our life in malice and envy, hateful, hating one another. But when the goodness and kindness of God our Savior and His love for mankind appeared [in human form as the Man, Jesus Christ], He saved us, not because of any works of righteousness that we have done, but because of His own compassion and mercy, by the cleansing of the new birth (spiritual transformation, regeneration)

and renewing by the Holy Spirit, whom He poured
out richly upon us through Jesus Christ our Savior,
so that we would be justified [made free of the guilt
of sin] by His [compassionate, undeserved] grace, and
that we would be [acknowledged as acceptable to
Him and] made heirs of eternal life [actually experi-
encing it] according to our hope (His guarantee).

—TITUS 3:3–7 (AMP)

Thank You, Everybody!

In everything give thanks; for this is the will
of God in Christ Jesus for you.

—1 THESSALONIANS 5:18

To Pastor Rick and Robin: Thanks for showing me that following Jesus doesn't mean you have to be uptight and serious. Like the time as a kid when I witnessed you eat pizza, give my dog a bite, and then take a bite yourself . . . changing my view of what a pastor could be.

To Pastor Dainsberg: For being willing to call me out in my sin, even if it didn't make me feel good. You weren't afraid and valued truth more than my feelings, so I could be set free.

To Grandpa Jim and Grandma Karen: For letting me tear your house apart countless times to shoot movies and skits in there, and for being my actors, willing or not. You encouraged me to be creative and let me use your house like a studio and your fridge like my grocery store.

To Grandma Pat: For being the matriarch of our family. At ninety-one years old, you set the standard for living a life close to Jesus. You've been a shining example of loving well and keeping a pure heart. Thanks for having a great sense of humor and showing us how to laugh and joke with purity as God intended us to.

To my mom, Jami: For praying for me constantly during my wild high school years. For boldly praying in my bedroom while I was at school that I'd come to know the Lord. It was in that very room I witnessed a miracle and came to know Jesus—changing my destiny for eternity.

To my dad, Dave: For being the best dad I could have ever imagined and giving us the perfect childhood. Thank you for answering my nine calls daily and walking me through decisions I'm about to make. For being a parent, friend, and counselor. For telling me to chase my dreams—even when I was ready to give up on them. You never stopped believing in me.

To Big Johnny, Ray, Devyn, Sean, and Clarence: For being an amazing community of friends for the last half decade. For lifting me up, helping me remain sold out and on fire for Jesus. For your rebukes, encouragement, and commitment to walking the road together. Your friendship matters more than you know.

To my brother-in-law, Walker: For encouraging me to always expand my dreams and vision and remain Kingdom-focused on every project we set out to do. For reminding me to never get comfortable, to constantly take ground for God, and to do everything in a Christ-like way.

And of course, to my loving wife, Mariana: For being the kindest, most loving woman in the world. For loving Jesus more than me and supporting me always. I love you.

Thank you to the Convergent team and the support staff for all of their help: Derek Reed, Theresa Zoro, Gail Gonzales, Leita Williams, Ashley Shoemaker, Steven Boriack, Elizabeth Groening, Claire Hendrix, Danielle Kolodkin, Cassie Gitkin, Jessie Bright, Jo Anne Metsch, and Vicky Lanzone. Thanks also to Bryan Norman and Alive Literary for your role in making this book possible.

And a heartfelt thanks to all the people who watch my videos and offer encouragement and prayers. And a super big thank-you to those who give. A lot of people keep showing up just because I ask them to. What a blessing. Without them, I'm just another guy on social media.

ABOUT THE TYPE

This book was set in Bembo, a typeface based on an old-style Roman face that was used for Cardinal Pietro Bembo's tract *De Aetna* in 1495. Bembo was cut by Francesco Griffo (1450–1518) in the early sixteenth century for Italian Renaissance printer and publisher Aldus Manutius (1449–1515). The Lanston Monotype Company of Philadelphia brought the well-proportioned letterforms of Bembo to the United States in the 1930s.